# Reflections on the War of the Willing

✦

*Frederic Rounds*

iUniverse, Inc.
New York   Bloomington

# Reflections on the War of the Willing

Copyright © 2008 by Frederic Rounds

iUniverse books may be ordered through booksellers or by contacting:

iUniverse
1663 Liberty Drive
Bloomington, IN 47403
www.iuniverse.com
1-800-Authors (1-800-288-4677)

ISBN: 978-0-595-52252-1 (pbk)
ISBN: 978-0-595-50977-5 (cloth)
ISBN: 978-0-595-62308-2 (ebk)

Library of Congress Control Number: 2008942285

Printed in the United States of America

# *Preface*

Since the beginning of the Bush administration, hundreds of books and articles have been written on foreign policy, intelligence, government, and the inner workings of the White House. Most, if not all, of the literature has been written by politically connected people: insiders, as it were. But, what are the rest of us thinking when a Congress essentially lets a president create an unmitigated disaster before the world's eyes. I have attempted to be one of your voices that belongs to the great masses of the unheard. I am as qualified to make a statement about the American political situation as any person who lives in the United States. I am not part of any political machine or action committee. I am one of you: those who are not elected, not privileged, and not politically influential. I merely took the opportunity to publish my daily thoughts in response to the evolving conditions in the world. I felt compelled to publish my journal because my government was certainly not speaking for me. I felt a need to express the views from the ordinary: a place we rarely hear from.

I spent six months of my life carefully watching the news as the Bush Administration led us into a war in Iraq. From the outset, I knew from my experience as a Vietnam Veteran that such a venture on the part of our government would be a mistake, because ultimately we would be trapped into another guerilla conflict far away from American shores. And the reasons for this war would not stand the test of time and truth. The Gulf of Tonkin incident was bogus. WMD also proved to be bogus.

The Iraq War started in March 2003. We now find ourselves in 2008 and the war continues. 2008 is also an election year with Republican John McCain and Democrat Barack Obama as presidential candidates. McCain says that we could be in Iraq for one-hundred years if necessary. Obama thinks troops will be out sixteen months after he takes office. I personally believe that whoever is elected President, the disposition of the Iraq War will be dictated by not only conditions in the region, but also by the driving political factors in America and the world. I believe neither of the presidential candidates would abandon Iraq, if the Iraqi government collapses. Right now I have little confidence that neither Obama nor McCain will bring American troops home any time soon. In addition to Iraq, I believe the conditions that the Bush administration will leave us are going to challenge all our abilities no matter who becomes president. Climate change, energy shortages, food and water shortages, healthcare, and record budget deficits will plague the twenty-first century for current and future generations. And, as I write this book, the fact that I am one of you indicates that we can have a voice. We can study the news and ask questions. Many of us who marched and spoke out against invading Iraq in early 2003 have proved themselves one-hundred percent correct in their thinking that an American adventure in Iraq would go wrong. Condoleezza Rice and John McCain called us uninformed and foolish respectively for staging such large protests. Obviously we now can look back and easily assess who were the real uninformed fools. Never again can we believe the myth that the government has the privileged position of knowing more than the American people.

The tools are available to allow everyone access to the information flow. The best source for this journal was the World Wide Web (WWW). The mainstream media in America proves to be limited and often biased. To obtain information, I found that sources from all over the world were essential, even to discover what was happening within our own country. The World Wide Web allows access to news from the most reputable international sources. Most of these news sources are from the mainstream press in not only America, but also Great Britain, Germany, France, Japan, Australia, and even the Middle East. In places where Americans were restricted from going, often foreign journalists could visit.

But, alas, the WWW has a few deficiencies. The Internet links (or universal resource locators [URL's] ) don't last forever. For any number of reasons, the Web sites from where the information was obtained may no longer exist even after a short span of time. Therefore, the many reference links that I have supplied may no longer be valid. I regret this displacement of such valuable information. Of course, with some effort the quoted data can be obtained by contacting the main source, such as *The Guardian, The Independent, The LA Times,* and so on. Probably you will be asked to pay for a copy from an archive. However, I trust that the information still exists. But in spite of the eventual access difficulties with WWW information, this electronic marvel is, in my mind, the greatest tool in protecting our freedom from tyranny which appears in the guise of propaganda, obfuscation, and false authority.

# Contents

# *January 5, 2003*

The Bush Administration makes me anxious. September 11th caused our country to be hyper-vigilant about terrorism, almost to the point of hysteria. But the greatest mania seems to come from the Bush Administration which declares that we are surrounded by an "axis of evil."

The image of this axis is causing a remarkable imbalance in our government's application of resources. North Korea has a well-developed nuclear technology and perhaps even a couple atomic bombs. Iraq doesn't seem to have any weapons of mass destruction, if we are to believe the UN inspectors. But the Bush Administration doesn't seem to believe the UN inspection results, and I don't believe the Administration. Nevertheless, all military forces are moving to the Middle East. We're acting like the war will begin sometime soon--February or March, 2003.

Our approach to North Korea is diplomacy. Rumsfeld believes we could go to war with both Iraq and North Korea simultaneously and defeat both "deliberately and decisively." Iraq is somehow a crisis; North Korea is not. The truth for me is America is in crisis. The crisis is our own disparity in moral values and processes. The world isn't a misbehaving child, as one might infer from the words coming from Washington. The threat of punishment from the skies has been shown to be a failure in Vietnam and Afghanistan. Yes, Afghanistan. Guerrilla attacks occur daily against coalition troops, including American. We respond with bombs from B-52s and hundreds of American troops. We find nothing. Multiple warlords control regions outside of Kabul. None of them agree with each other, and all of them have reputations of torture, abductions, and terror. Have we removed Osama bin Laden? No. Are we any safer from terrorism? No. Are we freer as a people? No. The Patriot and Homeland Security Acts have seen to that. The U.S. Congress has seen it politic to support a wild western president--unelected no less--in almost every resolution involving national security. I can't distinguish between Democrats and Republicans. And, the alternative parties present only a frivolous set of options.

# January 6, 2003

I'm a Vietnam veteran. So what? This possible distinction has brought me nothing in discourse or social status. I heard that World War Two veterans came home to free lunches, coffee, and job offers. This certainly wasn't the case for me.

Most people don't really understand what I did in Vietnam, since I was a naval officer. Most think I sailed about a safe distance from fighting. The truth of the matter is that I was assigned to riverine and coastal groups: small boats, junks, muddy rivers, defoliated river banks of the Mekong Delta, Viet Cong. I had a good dose of dysentery and malaria. We were supposed to stop the infiltration of weapons and supplies to the VC. The duty was dangerous and lonely. Often I was the only American on a junk with seven other Vietnamese sailors. I was supposed to advise the Vietnamese in the ways of naval warfare. John Paul Jones, however, didn't seem to fit into the situation. Americans in general didn't fit the mission in Vietnam. From my perception those who viewed the war from the John-Wayne mythology ended up dead or shut in air-conditioned hooches until their trick was up.

That was a long time ago for me, but Afghanistan hammers upon my brain as a constant reminder that America is now engaged in a repeat performance. I want to mention, however, that the name Colin Powell keeps coming up. Now he is the Secretary of State, but his name first came to my attention during the story of My Lai. In 1968 he was a major in the infamous Americal Division, the command that gave us My Lai. He was assigned to investigate the incident in which about 350 men, women, and children were murdered. Major Powell's investigation produced no evidence of an atrocity, and basically the case was dismissed, until more individuals later came forward to testify and a more concerted investigation was performed. Ultimately Lt. William Caley was found guilty of the My Lai massacre.

Now some say that Major Powell participated in a cover-up to avoid bad press for the Army--bad press for a bad war. I don't know whether the Army tried to intentionally cover up the story. I believe Powell could have legitimately believed he was performing all the necessary diligence to the investigation.

My Lai may have been one of the many reports of atrocities that were flying about during the Vietnam War. During one of my tours to Vietnam, I remember bombing a village not far from Vung Tau. Reports received from the spotters consisted of enemy killed-in-action, dead animals, destroyed watering areas, demolished structures, and denuded-tree areas. The whole bombing effort seemed quite indiscriminate to me. A salvo from a five-inch, thirty-eight cannon doesn't discriminate between men, women, and children. Perhaps Powell was merely numb as many of us were to the feelings that allow us to recognize an atrocity, especially when atrocities were all around us in Vietnam.

# January 7, 2003

I struggle trying to distinguish between Republicans and Democrats. They both support war with Iraq and they both talk about tax cuts. I imagine the Republicans lean harder for war and tax cuts for the rich. When all the arguments are done we'll see some type of tax cut that will be very small for low and middle-income citizens and probably a little more for people with high incomes. At any rate a tax cut doesn't make a lot of sense when we're trying to finance a war and we're already into deficit spending.

The last tax cut gave us about three-hundred dollars each. This meant nothing to me because I already owed about four-thousand dollars in taxes. But, did anyone really benefit significantly from the tax cut? The statistics from the Second Harvest Food Bank indicate that the number of people hungry in American is increasing. In 2001, 23.3 million Americans received food assistance from the Bank. That would be about one-tenth the population of the United States. Nine-million of those people were children. Thirty-six percent of those receiving food assistance were forced to choose between paying rent and eating.

Now the Bush Administration clearly states [http://usinfo.state.gov/topical/global/biotech/02/01601.htm] its commitment to end hunger. The focus has often been the starvation occurring in sub-Saharan Africa. Certainly to reduce world hunger is noble. I wonder though if we are fully aware of the hunger in America.

On December 24, 2002 the Washington Post reported that fundraising for food at the Capitol Food Bank was 30 percent behind projections. Shortages exist for many people who need assistance with their daily diets. And, this disparity exists right under the noses of our national leaders.

I find no compassion in these token tax cuts. If we can't feed our hungry, then what is the moral foundation for reducing taxes? I support increased taxes, if I can expect a balanced budget along with a balanced diet. Tax cuts please voters, however. The 23.6 million hungry people probably don't vote, so they don't count. They're disenfranchised. Perhaps the one percent of the population whose income is more than $300 thousand per year speaks louder in government halls than the greater masses. And, we note that Bush's tax package proposes to cut all taxes on dividends. The only people who make money off of dividends are the wealthy. Those workers who have their money tied up in 401K programs aren't taxed until retirement.

Hence, the dividend tax break has no immediate impact for most of us. The majority of Americans have no stock ownership whatsoever.

# January 8, 2003

I had a conversation yesterday with Nabil, the systems engineer working on our Windows 2000 upgrade. He's from Jerusalem and immigrated to America with his family at age 17. He's now 29 and married. He's also a devout Muslim. I was interested in relationships between Muslim women and men of other faiths.

About 6-million Muslims live in the U.S. and I know damn few of them. The number of Muslim women I've had extended conversations with is two. Both of these women wore the characteristic headscarf or hijab.

Anyway, Nabil clarified very emphatically that no Muslim woman would have a relationship with a non-Muslim, or infidel. Someone in the relationship would have to convert, or reject his/her religious rules. The first option might result in a loss of family ties, or the man would have to become a Muslim.

The latter option—becoming a Muslim—is, of course, a very acceptable option because many Muslims believe that Islam is the evolved form of Judeo-Christianity. A Muslim male apparently has an easier time marrying an infidel. Often, however, the spouse ultimately decides to adopt Islam rather than struggle with mixed religions.

Of course, from my standpoint, I react emotionally to these religious and cultural impositions. Freedom to act out the desire for love and courtship is restricted often through the vehicle of shame and rejection. The Muslims aren't the only group who has rules for interfaith marriage. Catholic priests generally will not perform interfaith weddings. With the status of Christian-based churches, however, many couples take a what-the-hell attitude toward the priest and go to a justice of the peace, or negotiate with a Protestant minister who doesn't have a problem with interfaith marriages.

My thought, however, is that non-Muslim men shouldn't attempt to develop a romance with a Muslim woman. I feel sad about this because my own belief is that relationships need to progress freely and that love needs to flourish without the fear of shame or rejection. I can see how conflict could easily develop, if our desires can only be met by joining a specific faith. Don't love and compassion transcend the precepts and rituals of a religion?

# January 9, 2003

I've been reading Scott A. Hunt's book, *The Future of Peace*. He interviews several of the great living peacemakers of the world, such as the Dalai Lama, Oscar Arias, Aung San Suu Kyi, and Maha Ghosanada. I have enormous respect for Mr. Hunt. His travels to so many parts of the world, and the personal risks he took are a triumph in journalism.

His message is most assuredly an important one in light of the current war tensions. Certainly the message that flows from all these great individuals is the idea of compassion as the leading component in peaceful interrelations.

For me compassion is a truth and something to always strive toward. I wish we all could think of compassion as the first component in our encounters with the world/universe.

I assume compassion is the basis of Maha Ghosanada's thoughts when he says:

> "We always remind the king to be in the present. He always thinks about the future, he always regrets the past, then he suffers. If he stays in the present moment, then he will be happy. Life is in the present moment. Breathing in, present moment, breathing out, present moment. We cannot breathe in the past, we cannot breathe in the future. Only here and now we can breathe. We always say, take care of the present moment. The present moment is the mother of the future. Take care of the mother, then the mother will take care of the children."

I react emotionally when I read the words from this renowned Cambodian Buddhist. I'm touched at various levels. Is this person spouting platitudes of some ambiguous religious dogma? Should I surrender to the obvious truths defined in the image of breathing? I choose a bit of the latter as I weave in the idea of compassion.

The past can be filled with regret. The future can be full of desires for material things and longing for conquest. The present, however, is the locus of action and the channel for compassion. The present contains our feelings that motivate our actions. Perhaps we must consciously feed and manage our feelings with compassion, so the outcome converges to a peaceful prospect. I say "prospect" because we cannot always know the consequences of our actions. Perhaps every breath in the present is a compassionate correction in the path weaving toward peace.

# January 10, 2003

The following are a couple of letters I wrote to the *San Jose Mercury News*. The second letter was published; the first was not. Both are examples of the campaign to keep the nation from going to war.

First Letter.

Editor, SJ Mercury News,

The fact that Iraq did not use biological or chemical agents on U.S. troops during the Gulf war indicates that Saddam Hussein in deterrable. The fact that the Scud missiles that landed on Israel and Saudi Arabia did not contain chemical weapons again indicates that Saddam is deterrable. Iraq doesn't have nuclear weapons, but may have some biological or chemical agents hidden someplace. This puts Iraq in the same category as twenty-five other countries, which avoid using weapons of mass destruction for fear of retaliation in kind. Hence, do we need to invade Iraq to disarm Saddam? Apparently some in our government think so because Saddam is an unpredictable maniac. However, logic fails me when we think about countries that contain weapons of mass destruction. By attacking preemptively we rid ourselves of the weapons and the maniac. By the same logic we should attack Canada because chemical weapons exist there and the country's leader might be a maniac now or at some unexpected time later—who knows. This same preemptive approach would necessarily apply to Britain, France, Russia,

South Africa, Pakistan, India, China, Iran, Australia, North Korea, Israel, the United States, and so on. There ought to be at least one maniac in this growing list of countries.

Second Letter:

Dear Editor, SJ Mercury,

When we receive these vague, open-ended, terrorist warnings, what are we supposed to do? Stay home? Avoid shipyards? Stop traveling? Stay out of high-rise buildings? Equip ourselves with gasmasks? Looks like we have the choice of doing whatever we think is necessary. Let's try peacemaking.

# *January 11, 2003*

So now North Korea has decided to pull out of the Nuclear Non-proliferation Treaty. The *San Jose Mercury News* reported today that the "Bush administration joined governments around the world Friday in strong condemnation of North Korea's decision to withdraw . . ."

I tried to find in the news article what governments around the world issued a strong statement.

Colin Powell says:

> "North Korea has thumbed its nose at the international community. This kind of disrespect for such an agreement cannot go un-dealt with. We're not going to be intimidated. We're not going to be put in a panic situation."

Dick Cheney says:

> "[The withdrawal would] undermine decades of non-proliferation efforts."

Of course, we need to keep in mind that the U.S. withdrew from the Antiballistic Missile Treaty.

Finally, we find in the article that the only other "condemnation" given by another national leader was Prime Minister Junichiro Koizumi of Japan:

> "We see this as a very serious matter."

I don't see "governments" condemning North Korea. I see one government, the U.S., exuding the bluster.

North Korea's leader, Kim Jong Il, seems to prefer to negotiate using a sledge hammer. The reaction of the Bush Administration is to return the favor with increased testosterone. With some feelings of guilt, I find myself taking Kim Jong Il's logic seriously.

The Bush administration has labeled North Korea as part of the Axis of Evil along with Iraq and Iran. Kim Jong Il sees the enormous military buildup and sanctions against Iraq. Iraq looks like the first one on the list of evil doers that is going to get "picked off" as it were.

[ "Picked off" are the words used by Bush in describing how we should deal with the sixty countries that harbor terrorists. See *Bush at War* by Bob Woodward. ]

Basically, Kim Jong Il sees a nuclear superpower about to dole out corrective action against evil doers. His response is to gear up in a way that he perceives will allow him to negotiate with equal footing.

North Korea has the third largest army in the world, a range of intercontinental ballistic missiles, possibly a few nuclear weapons, and other weapons of mass destruction. Kim Jong Il is saying he wants to negotiate with the U.S., but he does not want to be patronized and bullied by those with military superiority.

The U.S. response to North Korea's posturing is simply not to negotiate. Maybe we'll do some talking, but negotiating is out of the question. The administration has a ready-shoot-aim attitude in two other situations in which negotiations could have produced less costly results: Afghanistan and Iraq. Where is Osama bin Laden? Where is the end of terror? Where are the WMD? Do we feel safer with North Korea building nuclear weapons?

# January 12, 2003

I don't understand. In a Knight-Ridder survey published today in the San Jose Mercury, the following results appear:

> Question: Do you think Iraq and al-Qaeda—Osama Bin Laden's organization—are allied together to plan acts of terrorism, or not?

> Yes: 65 percent

> No: 16 percent

> Don't know/refused: 19 percent

I would answer "don't know" because no hard evidence exists from any source. So, why do 65 percent of the respondents feel certain that a relationship exists?

A purported meeting occurred between Iraqi agents and Muhammad Atta [ one of the 9/11 terrorists ], but this meeting has been refuted on a number of occasions. Muhammad Yousef, one of the perpetrators of the first World Trade Center bombing, was an Iraqi, but he was not associated with al-Qaeda to anyone's knowledge.

More likely is that these 65 percent are brainwashed by all the propaganda from the Bush Administration and the Media. No clear relationship may exist between Iraq and al-Qaeda. However, the fact that Iraq is Muslim, an 'evil-doer," a user of weapons of mass destruction, run by a maniacal despot, and under continuous world sanction may be what is on peoples' minds.

Evil associates with evil, I suppose. Since Iraq is a collection of very evil things, it must necessarily associate with al-Qaeda. The association may not have really existed. If these 65 percent were asked to present reasoning and factual evidence, my suspicion is that their position would be based on emotions: a confused amalgamation of fear, prejudice, and misinformation. My question to the 65 percent would be what evidence do they have of the Iraq-al-Qaeda connection? Simple. I haven't heard anything and I read the newspapers regularly. I've looked all over for the evil-doer connection. The only clear information I've found is that Saddam Hussein and Osama Bin Laden don't like each other.

The 65 percent seem to be willing to demonize very quickly. The 65 percent also seem to exist whenever a nationalistic fervor sweeps over a country. 65 percent would kill 6-million jews without thinking. 65 percent would kill innocent civilians, if the government and media create the right concoction of menace and evil.

However, 65 percent are the most important group of people in this country. They are the ones who will elect the government. We need them to ask questions. We need them for the world's salvation.

# January 13, 2003

What is "following your bliss" all about? How does one find his/her right livelihood? I have heard many popular psychologists proclaim that to bring joy into life a person must follow the dictates of the heart and not merely seek wealth, luxury, or material things.

I heard a radio show not long ago in which the commentator finally admits that we all need to do something to survive: food, shelter, and such. Of course, even though these basic elements are at the bottom of Maslow's pyramid, to attain them require a lot of effort, and time. Perhaps the pyramid is a wise construct because the base of it is much larger than the top, where life's spiritual components exist. The message is that we spend most of our time at the bottom. We expend most of our energy at the bottom simply caring for the things considered necessary for existence.

Of course, a lot of people have accumulated enough resources to allow them to spend their time in higher levels of pursuit. Apparently less than 1 percent of the American population earns sufficient income to allow them to avoid the worry of providing for the basics.

My son lives at the lower middle-income level for the San Francisco Bay Area. He shares rent with roommates to afford shelter. He owns a used car and rarely pays for regular maintenance. He reserves a small budget for entertainment. He isn't married, has no dependents, and dates very little. By in large his income provides room and board and not much else. He spends the greater part of the day earning his income. He does, however, work in a field that matches his interests. He could have opted to pursue a higher paying professions, such as business and engineering, but he chose ecology because the study followed his beliefs and temperament. I admire him for his diligence to his calling.

I chose to follow science, math, and engineering. I like these pursuits, but I enjoy them more as a hobby rather than as a profession. I make a living with computers and networks. I have made a good living, but I've always longed for something different. I'm not sure what exactly. I know often what I don't like. For example, I don't like the student's life of lectures and tests. I'm not a very good student, and sitting in a classroom is not far removed from torture.

Joseph Campbell tells us to listen to those quiet voices that reveal to us our bliss. He says we should follow these voices and urges without concern for money. Joseph Campbell does warn, however, that this journey through bliss is not without trial. The path belongs to heroes. So, if we select to travel down the road to "bliss", not only might we encounter trouble along the way, but also we might cause hardship for those with us: family, friends. Pretty damn scary.

# January 14, 2003

I sit here in my office watching asterisks crawl from left to right on my computer screen. [ Some types of system software let you know that things are working by sending an endless stream of asterisks across your computer screen. ] I'm trying to upgrade a piece of software on one of our communications switches. The ultimate goal is to make the switch run better and, thereby, improve performance, which would allow our enterprise to operate more efficiently and competitively. In spite of the amazing technology we live in, no electromechanical system is smart enough for humans to trust completely, nor are computers so independent that humans need not intervene occasionally to tune the mechanism. Sometimes I feel imprisoned within this vast machine. I watch the machine and feed it when required. I am the modern version of those who watched fire for their livelihood.

I don't feel natural sitting in my office behind a computer. I've been in this mode for almost thirty years. I've made a living by sitting behind a machine. I've never felt comfortable with having my fingers banging on a keyboard, or my arm trying to navigate a mouse. The feeling of discomfort is more like guilt. I am sinning against nature. I devote my mind to watching asterisks travel across a video display.

Realizing this kind of work is all for the greater good [a good which I don't fully see], I have sat imprisoned in my chair watching asterisks. "What's the alternative?" Some ask. Would I rather be running about the savannah chasing antelope? Or, would I rather be arranging dirt to squeeze out beans and corn? Days do go by in my life when I feel like a Luddite, and I should make every effort to be true to the Luddite philosophy. But, then I discover the World Wide Web as an answer to the drudging tasks of licking envelopes to pay bills, following the news from seven newspapers from around the world, renewing my driver's license, making travel reservations, and checking my bank balance.

Computers and networks have had a remarkable impact on our way of life. The development of this technology took years of effort from people like me: People willing to stare at a video display watching little glowing nits twitter about. But then after a long day is over, I go home and turn on my computer, read the email for today—much of it from antiwar groups, such as MoveOn and Answer. Maybe after this electronic social engagement, I'll watch a mindless series of TV shows on cable. I'm hoping something will really capture my interest. But, out of the 100-plus channels at my disposal usually nothing inspires me, but I continue watching and feeling somewhat guilty that I'm not reading, participating in community activities, planting a garden, or something other than mesmerizing myself in front of the TV.

My wife calls me away from the TV. She wants me to read with her. I resist, but I know she's right, so I force myself into the bedroom and try to read the best sellers, or the literature of the ages. But then I find that I've nearly expended my best hours watching asterisks. It's not long before sleep rescues me.

# January 15, 2003

Bush said yesterday:

> "The world came together, and we have given him [Saddam] one last chance to disarm. So far I haven't seen any evidence that he is disarming. Time is running out on Saddam Hussein—he must disarm. I'm sick and tired of games and deception."

When Bush speaks of the "world," he means the UN Security Council, which voted unanimously to check through inspection whether weapons of mass destruction (WMD) are still in Iraq. The plan is to check if Saddam has been compliant.

Bush is making the assumption that Saddam is lying when the dictator says that no WMD are in Iraq. The inspectors haven't found anything to date. So, Bush believes the Iraqis have hidden the WMD somewhere. The experts can't find them, so Bush must have information that no one else is privy to. Why doesn't the U.S. provide this information to the inspectors? I have heard no valid reason for holding back information.

I believe, however, that we don't have any specific information about the type and location of WMD in Iraq. If Bush and his advisers believe Iraq has WMD, even if the inspectors don't find any, then what's the point of inspections? Iraq is in material breach and we should let the war dogs slip, right?

The truth of the matter is we must be bluffing. We're putting heavy metal on the Iraqi borders, but this is only to put the squeeze on Saddam. The problem is that Saddam doesn't care. As was shown before, Saddam won't be intimidated: "If a country wants to invade, bring it on." Whatever the end result, the spin will be a mass atrocity brought about by the invading infidels. After the Gulf war, the atrocity of women and children dying certainly did occur due to sanctions, radioactive pollution by depleted uranium munitions, and destruction of civil utilities.

What does Washington's [I use *Washington* interchangeably with the *Bush Administration*] inconsistent and logically untenable behavior really add up to? Are we just trying to rid the Middle East of a terrible dictator? The answer from Washington has shifted from yes to basically no. The current reason is to disarm Saddam of WMD. If Saddam doesn't have WMD, then what? We would need to make up a story that claims Iraq has WMD no matter what anyone says. But, the "world" thinks the inspections need to reach some conclusion over this question. The end result is Bush losing all his reasons for attacking Saddam.

> "Iraq has a recent history of acquiring weapons of mass destruction and then using them to kill its neighbors, to invade countries, to bring attacks to others—Saudi Arabia, Kuwait, Israel, Iran," Mr. Fleisher said.

New York Times, January 14, 2003

Come on, Mr. Fleisher, get your history straight. Iraq used poison gas in the 1980's against the Kurds and the Iranians, not Kuwait, Israel, or Saudi Arabia. Iraq fired some short range, conventional-warhead missiles at Saudi Arabia and Israel during the Gulf war. These missiles were never classified as WMD.

Your comments are an insult, Ari, because you're misinforming the press and the public. You're leading people to believe things that aren't true. Remember also that Iran is a member of the axis of evil. During the 8-year Iran-Iraq war we supported Iraq and basically gave Saddam's army weapons training and intelligence. We even provided Iraq basic microbes to make biological WMD. We didn't make much of an issue of the atrocity that occurred when Iraq gassed Iranian troops—or the Kurds for that matter. The U.S. is complicit, Ari. If we are to try Saddam Hussein for war crimes, then we'll need to stand up there with him.

# January 16, 2003

I am debating whether to march in San Francisco on Saturday. I marched before, but first, the event was very peaceful and, second, almost every cause was represented, not just those against the Iraq war.

One person approached me and claimed that the military had developed technology to control the weather. Apparently global warming is a covert scheme to shift weather patterns so as to weaken a particular region, such as California or New York. Also, I noted signs for gay rights, freeing Tibet, protecting the arctic wilderness, and so on. In the midst of the parade the Green party's gubernatorial candidate rolled down Market Street in a pickup truck.

I read today in the www.telegraph.co.uk that the White House has "reassured" Senate Republicans that the evidence exists for Iraq's possession of WMD. Not only does the evidence exist, according to the White House, but so does also a definite connection to al-Qaeda.

Why would the White House want to deal with information in this way? By alluding in the press that we know something would only result in Iraq's increased care in hiding the weapons.

I would imagine a better approach would be to feed this information to the inspectors and have them find it. This secrecy just leads my mind into suspicions that we don't have any such evidence at all, or if we do, the information is meaningless. Why does Bush remind me of Captain Queeg from *The Caine Mutiny?*

> "Ah, but the strawberries! That's where I had them. They laughed at me and made jokes, but I proved beyond the

shadow of a doubt, and with geometric logic, that a duplicate key to the wardroom icebox did exist! And I'd have produced that key if they hadn't pulled Caine out of action!"

Humphrey Bogart as Captain Queeg
Caine Mutiny

Queeg may be the characterization of the collective Bush, Card, Rove, Rumsfeld, Cheney, Wolfowitz, Perle, et al. These missing strawberries are the WMD hidden in Iraq. The "key" to finding the strawberries exists somewhere in the minds of the collective. But, political pressure from the world has taken "Queeg" out of action, so the "key" can't be produced right this very moment, but if given the chance, the world, according to the collective, will surely realize the very "sanity" of this issue.

# January 17, 2003

The UN inspectors found 12, 122mm empty chemical rounds yesterday. Who manufactured the munitions? Russia, Egypt, China, North Korea? Iraq has admitted that they were imported. None of the stories so far has revealed where these arms came from. But, we know Iraq doesn't manufacture this type of weapon. Therefore, some country sold Iraq weapons designed to spread chemical agents.

Now we can take this WMD information and play it up in the spin factory. We can be led to think that Iraq is now assuredly in material breach. I have full confidence that maximum mileage will be made of these munitions, even though they were empty and unusable. I recall though that the Tonkin Gulf incident was equally small and ambiguous, but ultimately the naval event became so exaggerated that President Johnson went to war over it.

This munitions discovery leads to questions regarding the involvement of the U.S. intelligence. Apparently the inspectors are receiving help from U.S. intelligence agencies. Was this latest find a product of intelligence relationship with the inspectors? If so, then the information so far does not feel very compelling. Twelve empty shells imply not much more than nothing. Maybe a plan existed at one time to use these shells for attacking U.S. troops. But, the munitions weren't situated in a cocked and ready position. They were in a dump.

Recently the UPI ( Richard Sale ) reported that Israel is planning to step up its programs of assassinations by enlarging the Mossad ( Israel's Intelligence Agency ) terrain to include the United States. I wonder whom the Mossad might consider an enemy. But, why not? We entered Yemen with a Predator drone and assassinated Qaed Salem Sinan al Harethi, apparently an al-Qaeda leader.

Tomorrow is the big protest day in San Francisco. The ANSWER organization is a major leader in putting the event together. We should note that the core values of ANSWER are based on a Marxist-Leninist philosophy: communism. The *Mercury News* made a point of this connection today, which I'm sure will throw cold water on the show in San Francisco. Most people have never heard of ANSWER and could care less about its core values. My question is: are we being duped by ANSWER? ANSWER has never said anything negative about Saddam or Kim Jong Il. However, I am glad that ANSWER has stepped up to organize this protest.

# January 19, 2003

We didn't go to the peace march yesterday. Apparently the crowd was large and the press made a front-page story about it. ( See the *Mercury News.* ) The press covered this protest much more than it did last October. The first unprecedented Iraq war protest received no real press coverage at all.

The *Mercury News* reported that a Bush spokeswoman said, "People in the United States, unlike Iraq, are free to protest and to make their case known." Of course, we had news reports yesterday that 1000 Iraqis marched in support of their government and against a U.S. invasion. We also heard of marches taking place all over the world in opposition to a war.

WMD are a trap. Using them creates an irreparable disaster. Hence, WMD are a deterrent for the *sane.* For the *insane,* using WMD is suicide under most circumstances. Of course, the exception exists with Saddam Hussein himself, who has a history of using WMD against the Kurds and Iranians. The U.S. looked the other way at the time because we were engaged in trying to eliminate the Iranian leadership. The U.S. has a flexible morality when circumstances so dictate: atomic bombs during WW II, the cold-war construction of the world's largest WMD arsenal, the tacit approval of chemical weapons deployment during the Iran-Iraq war.

How does a country get itself into such quagmires as Vietnam and Iraq? I don't see dots connecting information that would lead to a compelling story for war. I'm reading that Washington is currently building an argument, but no one is expecting a smoking gun. I understand that a collection of facts will be gathered which will show a pattern of "material breaches." Do material breaches imply war? Our administration seems to think so, but the public is resistant. Somehow around 50 percent of the public believes we should go after Saddam as long as we go in with UN sanction and a coalition. Bush will likely try to put such a coalition together, just as his Father did. If he doesn't get the support, then there will be no war. The troops will come back. We will not hold the crisis open indefinitely. Or, am I thinking wishfully?

# January 20, 2003

The White House is now considering the possibility of exile for Saddam Hussein. Of course, most suspect Saddam would never abdicate his power and leave. He's too wedded to his country. I don't understand how a man with his brutal history could find the support to stay in power. Apparently 20 percent of the population has left for asylum in other countries.

Joe Stork [*Progressive*, January, 2003] provides a detailed account of the many atrocities and affects of Saddam's rule:

1) 700,000-1,000,000 people displaced;

2) citizen politics criminalized;

3) The murder of about 100,000 Kurds in 1988;

4) southern marshes drained as part of a counter-insurgency plan;

    (The UN claimed this to be one of the world's greatest environmental disasters.)

5) 120,000 Kurds expelled from the oil-rich Kirkut region.

The interesting note is that very little has been published in the U.S. about Saddam's expulsion of Kurds from the Kirkut region. The fact that Saddam now controls this area creates significant booty for the conqueror. Would the U.S. allow the displaced to return to their homeland, or would this be another story much like that of the Native Americans? Are we experiencing a conscious suppression of the news? I can easily imagine that most people in the U.S. have never heard of the Kirkut region. Would Kirkut be a regular part of the White House's Iraq discussion? I doubt it. Certainly though, the oil explorers would likely track the oil sources of the world. We don't know whether Kirkut feeds the motivation for war. I don't find the popular arguments for an oil war very convincing.

I find myself looking at the big picture, obsessed with preventing this war in Iraq, rather than caring about the things and people in my neighborhood. The consequence of looking only at the big picture and rejecting the neighborhood is that the things that the single individual can do simply don't get done.

I note that the empty 122mm chemical rounds found in Iraq were supplied by Egypt and Italy. So is Iraq the only member of the grand coalition of badness?

# January 21, 2003

Notice these letters from two different newspapers:

**The Ledger Online ~ Serving Central Virginia**

**President Bush is delivering the right proposal at the right time.**

Dear Lynchburg Ledger:

When it comes to the economy, President Bush is demonstrating genuine leadership. ...

Sincerely,

Derick Mfoafo

Lynchburg, VA

**Bush shows leadership**

[Letter to Green Bay Press-Gazette – People's Forum]

APPLETON - When it comes to the economy, President Bush is demonstrating genuine leadership....

Edward T. Kranick

Yes, they are both the same, but they have different senders. I was able to find thirteen newspapers around the country that carried this same letter all with different senders.

I have learned that this letter originated from a Republican Party website [www.gopteamleader.com]. Once you become a member or team leader, you have the privilege of blast emailing the same letter to a wide variety of recipients. Apparently this email spammer attaches bogus names to the letter, so we experience what may appear to be a very wide following on a political issue.

I haven't made an in depth study of this spam approach in politics, but I can imagine that both major parties and other organizations have web-based tools to allow mass emailing to a list of recipients. Perhaps some of these tools attach different originators to the mail.

I looked in the Lynchburg, Virginia directory for a Derick Mfoafo and couldn't find any such name, or anything close to it. The name looks a little unusual.

Now how do I feel about this mass email? Is it spam? Yes. Do I like spam? No. Is it propaganda? Yes. Do I like propaganda? No. Is it deceitful? Yes. I don't like to be deceived. I wonder if some sort of deceptive practice that leads us to believe in a certain way biases some of the opinion polls.

A year has passed since our war in Afghanistan began. The power distribution consists of Kabul and competing regional warlords. The U.S. and other nations haven't fully delivered $4.5 billion in aid, so Karzai [Kabul's/quasi-Afghanistan's president] can't extend his power much beyond the city's borders.

Apparently the Taliban and al-Qaeda now are surviving in Pakistan. Bin Laden seems to have escaped, even though the greatest army in the world has been hunting for him. So the question remains: has the war in Afghanistan been successful? Perhaps we can make an argument that certain types of successes have occurred, such as improvements in the economy of Kabul and more openness in women's rights. Could these achievements be provided by a means other than war? Maybe, but we definitely would have needed to negotiate with the Talaban. Similarly we may have been able to secure Bin Laden through negotiation. Instead we proceeded to intimidate via the threat of military force. So far, the end result of war has been death, destruction, some rebuilding, and no real stability. Afghanistan has returned as the largest producer of heroin. We have Vietnam all over again. Iraq would most assuredly end up the same way.

# January 22, 2003

The White House released a document called the *Apparatus of Lies*: No author, no date. This document is supposed to convince world leaders of Iraq's pervasive history of lying and deceptions. Unfortunately I found hardly any new information within the 30 pages of old stories. The document is 32 pages long. No evidence exists of stockpiles of WMD, except for 16 empty warheads.

The paper talks about using human shields to protect military equipment in the event that the U.S. strikes. What it doesn't say is that many of the shields are in Iraq as volunteers--such as Voices in the Wilderness—with full intentionality of being used as shields.

The paper says that Saddam uses the oil for food program to line his pockets and build castles and weapons, rather than feed the people. Saddam blames the sanctions for starvation. While misuse of the UN oil-for-food program is a fact, the sanctions have had no positive benefit for the people of Iraq. Sanctions do not help the flow of food, medicine, and other products. And, starvation was not a significant problem before the sanctions were installed.

The document notes "ongoing intimidation of Iraqi scientists," but no further description is provided.

The document asserts:

> "Numerous chemical, biological, and nuclear weapons stockpiles and programs unaddressed in the Iraqi declaration."

What does this statement mean? Do WMD stockpiles exist, but are not declared? Are some of the known older, destroyed, and/or abandon stockpiles not declared?  Apparently we know something, but are unwilling or unable to convey this information to the expert inspectors for clear verification.

Finally, the document says that Iraq is not providing "active" cooperation with the UN inspectors.  So, Iraq is providing passive cooperation.  I imagine passive cooperation is better than no cooperation.  The possibility from my perspective is that Iraq may have revealed all they know.  I could imagine that a search of the massive amount of military hardware in a government's possession would reveal substantial accounting errors and oversights.  If areas have been bombed or disrupted in the past, accountability may become extremely difficult.  I can imagine what might happen if we audited the weapons storage depots of the U.S. military.  Would we be able to account for everything?  Would we find some evidence of disrepair?  Stories have appeared occasionally of leaks in the chemical weapons at the Rocky Mountain Arsenal.

Now the most damning problem with this document is the reference to depleted uranium.  The paper mentions that the World Health Organization, the UN Environment Program, and the European Union "could find no health affects linked to exposure of depleted uranium."  This statement alone might lead a person to think that spreading uranium into the environment is just fine.  We note that the UN Environmental Program (UNEP) clearly advises precaution in dealing with depleted uranium.  See:

www.iaea.org/worldatam/Press/Focus/DU/finalreport.pdf

> "...the results suggested that there is no immediate cause for concern regarding toxicity.  However, major scientific uncertainties persist over the long-term environmental impacts of DU, especially regarding ground water.  Due to these uncertainties, UNDP call for precaution..."

With most propaganda the important action for the reader is to check the sources to get the full story.  Just a cursory look at the UNEP report does confirm the lack-of-harmful-evidence claim as depicted in the White House document.  However, UNEP goes on to clarify that "major" uncertainties exist particularly the long term effects.

One of the first rules of propaganda is to present a factual part of a story: just enough to sound convincing.  The White House paper does a reasonable job at meeting this rule, but the bottom line is the White House seems to be doing the same thing as Baghdad:  deceiving, distorting, and lying.  What drives an elected government to engage in these desperate activities?  Read John Fialka's article in the *Wall Street Journal*.  He may be right in claiming that no definitive harmful effects occur because of DU, but he also clearly states the long term uncertainties.

# January 23, 2003

The White House, among others, does have information unknown to the general public that clearly indicates that Saddam Hussein has not been forthright in his 12000-page accounting of weapons of mass destruction (WMD). Recall that the U.S. received the initial copies of the report and then disseminated an edited version to the UN. The information that was edited is obviously sensitive data about where a good bit of the WMD came from. The sources listed below suggest that the U.S. carefully removed WMD suppliers from Iraq's disclosure documents. Apparently the list of enterprises is extensive and pervasive through both commercial and government sectors: Hewlett Packard, DuPont, Honeywell, Rockwell, Tectronics, Bechtel, International Computer Systems, Unisys, Sperry and TI Coating, U.S. Departments of Energy, Defense, Commerce, and Agriculture, Lawrence Livermore, Los Alamos and Sandia National Laboratories. [ see, for example, http://www.interex.org/hpworldnews/hpw302/news7.jsp, or http://66.102.7.104/search?q-cache:Wa7r2H5wjeYJ:www.annesummers.com.au/smh0302.pdf+iraq+disclosure+document+hewlett+packard+guardian&hl=en ] Argument exists over what these companies actually supplied to the Iraqis: if not actual WMD, then dual use technologies.

Of course, the U.S. was not the only supplier of WMD to Iraq: France, Italy, Egypt, Germany, and Russia were also involved. These weapons trades occurred during the Iran-Iraq war primarily. At the time the U.S. had diplomatic relations with Iraq because we were trying to instigate a regime change in Iran. Iraq used gas warfare extensively against Iran and others, causing horrific casualties. Little vocal outcry came from the U.S. government at the time. Wonder why? [See http://yt.org/article.php?sid=1007]

This selective editing seems very logical to me in light of the White House's general behavior in revealing the basis for the current U.S. obsession with Iraq. I would imagine that revealing such information would be extremely damaging to U.S. credibility, since some of this poison trading occurred during the Reagan-Bush Sr. years.

However, I have considerable doubt that anything that I've said above will reach front-page news, or will ever be confirmed by solid news sources because any company admitting to supplying WMD to Iraq would be culpable in the banned weapons conspiracy.

# January 24, 2003

The Bush Administration appears now to be under considerable pressure to join the international community in slowing down the run to war. The French and Germans decided to just say no, and let the inspectors complete their mission. China and Russia look like they are doing the same thing. Senator John Kerry (Democrat, Massachusetts) is calling Bush's behavior "bluster for war." Even some Republican senators are asking Bush to slow down.

Rumsfeld is getting considerable criticism for calling France and Germany "old Europe." Perhaps he implied that new Europe complies with everything the U.S. wants, even waging war without full clarity of reason and purpose. The Bush Administration appears to be isolating itself into the White House. It doesn't seem to have a good pulse on what's happening on all continents. Do the military forces feel obligated to support another war? Generals should resign, I suppose, if they don't agree with the Commander in Chief. You'd think that people watching the world would wonder what all the to-do is about. Why aren't we asking more questions? Where is Congress in the issue of a war with Iraq? Why is Congress so silent?

# January 26, 2003

I was torn from my hobbies and housework yesterday to help fix our school district's data network. I didn't get home until 11:15pm. This is the plight of working in a utility profession. We're always on call. Our lives can be interrupted by the failure of the great machine.

The machines are our life support. We become slaves to their care and feeding. They are our children born from our minds. Machines are like money. We think that the more machines we have, the greater will be our power and influence over nature and our productive capacity. Yet, for some, more machines simply implies more work in keeping those machines well oiled. For others, machines have resulted in disenfranchisement. I often wonder whether our age of automation has actually resulted in less toil in our lives.

If a machine produces the exact same amount of products as the equivalent collection of human workers doing the same task, then theoretically people would end up with more time. Machines, however, produce a great deal more of the final product, but the result is not necessarily the reduction of labor, but rather a transfer of labor to people with a different collection of skills. Such is the unusual aspect of the 20th/21st century workplace.

People are cast into factories and work at very specific jobs, such as attaching a component to an engine, or soldering a wire to a circuit board. As technology improves jobs are displaced and the obsolete-skilled labor either needs to retrain or go hungry. This industrial system is often doomed to failure because no safety net exists for those disenfranchised.

In theory capitalism can provide livelihood for a large number of people, but the concurrent social system is not set up to guarantee a minimal set of services, such as health care, shelter, and food. These services are most easily available if you're working within the capitalist system. Capitalism has helped millions of people obtain good livelihood, perhaps at the expense of millions whom are disenfranchised by the bottom line salary/profit balance.   We expect government to take over when the private sector fails to fill our social needs. Yet, often those who operate the elected government are the same people who run the capitalist economy.  Is it possible that by mixing together the capitalist and political minds we inhibit our ability to care for the general welfare of the disenfranchised?

# January 27, 2003

We were successful in bringing our network back into functional order. The human effort was large and dedication to machine life was high. We didn't receive any thanks for the work: just a lot of frustrated telephone callers. What does it all mean?

In spite of all the nay-sayers about a war with Iraq, Bush still presses ahead with rhetoric. The President says, "Iraq [ Saddam ] has not proven his disarmament. He's [ Saddam ] is a liar." Probably half of the American people aren't buying Bush's rhetoric. People want something that truly allows them to feel comfortable with war. The information must be sufficient to raise the visceral juices to kill people whom we don't know. The reason for war must be compelling, such as an unprovoked attack on our country or possibly our allies. We haven't seen any sort of attack from Saddam Hussein, and the Bush administration is having a hard time finding a convincing threat from Iraq.

So what if Saddam is lying? What if he is hiding weapons of mass destruction? Do these facts justify war? I would say no. If, however, we found solid evidence that Iraq had supplied terrorists with illegal weapons, then we would need to apprehend the terrorist. We actually wouldn't have any choice but to apprehend the terrorist because attacking Iraq directly would likely create a mood within the Iraqi government to justify the use of WMD.

The bottom line is I don't know the best approach to take with Iraq. I do know that war is not an option at all. The ideas described above about going after terrorists sounds all well and good, but the process would be very difficult as shown in the case of Bin Laden. Probably the most optimized way to deal with Saddam is the one that was put in place after the first Gulf War: sanctions and inspections. I wonder how much the nations that surround Iraq could do to help manage Saddam. Apparently, however, the Saudis, Jordanians, and Syrians are not particularly worried about Saddam's WMD.

# January 28, 2003

Bush gave his State of the Union message tonight. Most of it was well written and crafted for his voice quality and personal manners. He's certainly capable of giving a good address in front of the entire world. But, I feel strongly that his speaking skill may be his only respectable quality because his content was also crafted to not only sound good, but also deceive: superb propaganda. Perhaps the speech could be classified as a quiet man's version of Adolph Hitler—a quiet fury of looming tyranny.

Of course, he spoke of tax cuts, but not how he will deal with the exploding deficit. He spoke of Medicare, but he did not mention the plan for an HMO-plus-Medicare program. He spoke of environmental programs, but we all know his record of nearly eliminating twenty years of environmental advances and programs.

He provided little new evidence of Iraqi transgressions with weapons of mass destruction. He even mentioned the infamous aluminum tubes again, even though scientific authorities know that these tubes have nothing to do with nuclear centrifuges or any other nuclear system. The fact that the President would misuse such information so nonchalantly puts his whole argument in jeopardy.

The American people were deceived tonight and I don't have the confidence that we will bother to ask the necessary questions. Without our knowing we shall be thrust into a war. People will die.

I feel Bush set this course toward war with Iraq. Yet, I don't understand the administration's motivations. I don't really understand the world's motivation. France seems opposed to a U.S. unilateral attack, but France has also hinted that she may turn a blind eye if she can have oil rights.

But, what is my great problem with Bush? Why am I so obsessed with him as a political problem? First, I feel powerless to do anything about the world situation. I have no avenues to express my ideas. And, I don't feel heard by many. My voice is silent. I write letters to editors and congressional representatives. Senator Boxer seems sympathetic. Senator Feinstein seems to be becoming a Republican more and more. I think she should change parties. Perhaps all I can really do is try to comfort others: try to help where I can; talk to people who are fearful.

# *January 29, 2003*

"…and many others have met a different fate. Let's put it this way: they are no longer a problem to the United States and our friends and allies."

Bush<br>
State of the Union<br>
1/28/03

What kind of President would use such language with such impunity and nonchalance? Perhaps his obsession with Iraq is based on a fear that he sees himself in Saddam Hussein.

> "Our intelligence sources tell us that he [Hussein] has attempted to purchase high-strength aluminum tubes suitable for nuclear weapons production."

Bush<br>
State of the Union<br>
1/28/03

The inspectors have clarified that these tubes are not designed for nuclear weapons production. Why does Bush continue to use this misleading information when those who read and watch the news know better? If Bush doesn't know the correct information, then how can he be fit to make a rational judgment, especially regarding war?

> "…US intelligence indicates that Saddam Hussein had upwards of 30,000 munitions capable of delivering chemical agents. Inspectors recently turned up 16 of them…Saddam Hussein has not accounted for the remaining 29,984…"

Bush
State of the Union
1/28/03

What does "upwards of 30,000" mean? Does this mean equal to 30,000? Does this mean approximately 30,000? What should we really be looking for here: 30,000- 16, or 29,984? Or, are we expecting upwards of 29,984? How do we know that the munitions found in the Iraqi bunkers are part of the same batch Bush is talking about? How do we know what timeframe Bush is referencing? Perhaps the 30,000 munitions were obtained 20 years ago.

Bush makes no case for a war. His evidence is just a collection of trumped up propaganda. If this garbage can sway America, then we have no hope of rising above the fear and mania that Bush seems to want to awaken in us. We must do all that's possible to remove this artificial nightmare from government.

# *January 30, 2003*

"...one power with a president who has no foresight, who cannot think properly, is now wanting to plunge the world into a holocaust."

Nelson Mandela
CNN
Jan. 30, 2003

"The President will understand there are going to be people who are more comfortable doing nothing about a growing menace that could turn into a holocaust. He respects people who differ with him. He will do what he thinks is right and necessary to protect our country."

Ari Fleischer
CNN
Jan. 30, 2003

I sit in silence wondering about what may come in light of all the madness so demonstrated by the words above. Though I agree with Mandela, by demeaning a national leader, he leaves himself open for an equivalent retort. Perhaps we shall offer Saddam the option of exile. But, I think everyone realizes at this point that Saddam would never hear of such a thing. Hence, this offer is only a political masquerade that adds into the fantasy that America did everything possible to avoid war, except just not to have one.

# *January 31, 2003*

How is it possible that I could become a member of both the Republican and Democratic (senatorial) campaign committees? I have been asked many times to contribute to the Democrats because I am a Democrat. I have never been asked to join the Republican National Committee. I probably ended up on some mailing list and the Republicans are trying valiantly to insure enough popular votes for the next election. I can predict without much effort that what happened in 2000 will not happen in 2004. The popular vote certainly had the right result when America gave Al Gore the election. The Electoral College in one of those rare circumstances was compelled to appoint Bush. Of course, the Supreme Court helped by stopping the litigation and vote counting in Florida.

So we have an unelected president carrying the nation off to a war about which most people in the world have significant misgivings about. Bush also continues efforts to lower taxes when the national deficit continues to increase.

Apparently Prime Minister Tony Blair is right now trying to convince Bush to get another reading from the UN Security Council before starting a war. Of course, UN disapproval would be Blair's way out of the fight without losing too much face. Bush, on the other hand, would be abandoning international sanction, unless he can convince the UN to vote approval.

Blair has little support in England for this war. He has a lot to lose, if he goes off to war with the U.S. and a few other allies. He may just get himself voted out, especially if something goes wrong.

Of course, the question is how the military would attack a city of six-million like Baghdad. We could bomb it to rubble, which would damage many archeological treasures. We could fight house-to-house. This technique would torture many innocents.

# *February 2, 2003*

Yesterday at about 9:00am the space shuttle Columbia exploded upon reentry. I retired from NASA about six years ago. I remember when the Challenger blew up on takeoff. It took three years to get back into space again. Now that we have people living in space, I doubt if we can afford to wait for another three years before we figure out what happened and what we can do about it.

The way I understand this mishap is that a piece of the launch vehicle broke off upon takeoff. The piece fell back into the left wing. Apparently no damage appeared until the shuttle reached the upper atmosphere. Columbia is one of the oldest shuttles and I believe we should have expected a problem, especially after the left wing had been hit. We need to think of better ways to escape calamity with our space exploration. Yet, until we find better ways of space travel, our current program will likely die away. Space will have a vacation from us for a while.

We only have three shuttles left. Bush doesn't appear bent on increasing the NASA budget. So perhaps we're now entering a long dry spell for exploration.

I went to the bookstore today. Nothing really spoke to me. I was searching for some new ideas other than those of an angry pacifist or a hawk. I will say that I found more pacifists than hawks, which must be a good sign.

I would like to see our Administration do something unique and daring, such as pay a personal visit to Saddam and negotiate a deal. Instead he falls in line with all the other despots throughout the ages. The media around me presents an empty message: an unimaginative idea drawn from the annals of historic precedent. Hit the other guy with a club, or we've used every possible diplomatic option, except discussion and negotiation. With Bush I see a person not capable of intelligent negotiation. Rumsfeld actually met and spoke with Saddam Hussein during the 1980's. This Administration seems totally rejecting, unimaginative, macho, and arrogant.

# February 5, 2003

After Secretary Powell's presentation before the UN, I wrote the following message to the *SJ Mercury*:

> We've seen Secretary Powell deliver to the UN a collection of raw intelligence. Intelligence is information gathered from a distance and out of context. It requires verification and extensive analysis. Often intelligence can easily be incorporated into a propaganda program because of the ease of multiple interpretations. A classic example of propaganda is Powell's first piece of evidence, a captured telephone conversation:
>
> > Gen: "You didn't get a modified. . .
> > "You don't have a modified. . ."
>
> Powell leads us to conclude that the general is talking about a weapon of mass destruction. However, we see no mention of any weapons at all. What is a "modified..."? Our government is trying to convince the world that we need to go to war. Listen critically to what is being said. Ask questions? Demand verification and inspection. And, most of all, Saddam probably does have weapons of mass destruction salted away. Should we go to war over this? If yes, then we probably should go to war with the twenty-four other countries that possess weapons of mass destruction.

Bear in mind that I don't get many of my letters published. I pray that people will listen carefully and critically to what was said. Powell's presentation was convincing and powerful, yet it was deeply troubling in that the supposed revelations are much like the examples shown above. The suggestions were ominous, but we actually were told very little. We still don't have hard evidence, except that we can't seem to find anything that we claim Iraq has.

I have little doubt that Iraq is hiding some weapons of mass destruction, but the obvious truth is Saddam hasn't used them since before the Gulf war, and who used what when between Iran and Iraq remains unclear or poorly reported.

Also, Powell brought up the aluminum tubes again, even though the inspectors have deemed them not designed for nuclear enrichment. Hence, the U.S. has established a basic disagreement with the UN. Therefore, the truth regarding these tubes remains uncertain and inconclusive. How can we possibly justify a war without making an absolute case? I suppose some people for whatever reason don't require a lot of basis for war. Some don't want war for any reason. Our country appears to lean toward the former type of thinking.

The *SJ Mercury* published a story today about the growing number of county and city governments that are voting for resolutions against an Iraq war. The County of Santa Clara is one of these governments. Sixty-four cities across America have adopted resolutions. I personally have suggested a resolution for Sunnyvale, California, but I have not received a response, nor has Sunnyvale acted in any way regarding the war or the Patriot Act.

I find this local government tactic of adopting resolutions regarding national policy to be something new on the political scene. As cities go, then possibly so go the states. If the states present resolutions, then possibly the federal government will do the same. This cascade of resolutions would indeed be a grassroots form of government.

As a feeling note, today was a dark day for America when a senior government official [ Colin Powell ] went before the world and presented exaggerated and unprocessed information for the sole purpose of fomenting a war. Hitler's reasons for executing Jews were based on the dictator's deviant and seriously deluded mind. What's happening in government now reminds me of an unstoppable train filled with characters swarming in Dante-like infernal madness.

# *February 6, 2003*

I interpret what people say along the lines of a certain prejudice, especially if I feel antagonistic to a point of view. Obviously I'm against a war with Iraq under any circumstances. When Powell presented his arguments, I rejected them based on grounds of verifiability and logic. Using these grounds nothing of what Powell said holds up. Of course, I'm taking a position of suspicion and mistrust. Politicians lie. In the case of war, politicians lie even more. However, I need to feel convinced that war is a necessity. I haven't been convinced of any wars' necessity since World War II.

I feel frustrated when Senator Feinstein lauds the President and Secretary of State for such a fine job in justifying the need for war. She insults my intelligence and I'm not very intelligent. If I can see credibility issues in an argument, then why can't our Senators.

I imagine propaganda affects peoples' ears in different ways. Some—perhaps many—will be swept up in the words; some will not. I don't want to listen to propaganda. I don't want to feel duped, and I don't want to go to war with Bush in the lead.

The only people who speak critically are those who might be called leftists: Phyllis Brennis, Bob Fisk, Dan Ellsberg, and so on. I guess the positive message is that the Administration appears to make all the right moves with the UN. Unfortunately Bush and company continue with the tough bravado. Not many like macho talk, and I suppose the world reacts to the machismo more than a substantial argument. Bush simply talks like a bully. He doesn't seem to respond to large popular feedback.

I sincerely think he believes his own propaganda and he is willing to go to war over circumstantial evidence.

But credibility lapses exist throughout Bush's plans for war.  The President put no money for an Iraq war in his budget proposal.  What a glaring oversight.  I'm thinking that the war talk is nothing but a hoax to bring Saddam in line.  If we really plan to start a war, then we won't be able to afford it.

# February 7, 2003

War seems imminent, so my wife and I took off for the mountains together. We needed to get away from the constant barrage of war talk, bluster, and even frantic cries for a peaceful resolution.

As we travel, however, I note a strange drop in ski tourism. This has been a low snow year—a draught. But I can see snow in the mountains. I sense that people are overwhelmed with work, or perhaps no work. Skiing cost a virtual fortune. I don't go downhill skiing anymore. I've gotten into cross-country. But groomed trails are now about half the price of downhill and I've seen an exploding market in stylish backcountry skiwear comparing well with downhill fashions. Snow recreation has become a style that fewer people can afford. I find the expense and accoutrements of some sports and recreation cause these activities to lose meaning and purpose. But such is my prejudice. The world doesn't revolve around my prejudices and beliefs.

Perhaps as I am surrounded by the mountain's frozen immensity, I easily believe the government's case for fomenting a war at this moment in history seems completely absurd. Yet, a large body of people—perhaps half the U.S. population—believe the righteousness of our government and the absolute need to battle Saddam Hussein. What I think represents only a miniscule pressure against a gorilla of a system. I feel the move to war is unstoppable. I make my notes and protests, but the world goes on without me. I can only pray. Prayer is a form of asking a greater power to intervene. But what happens when the power doesn't intervene? Does God's non-intervention refute the existence of this higher power? Or, does the greater power move the outcome of events in a direction contrary to my desires? I agree actually with the latter because God has a grander more complex plan for the universe: a scheme beyond my comprehension. Death—perhaps appearing terrible and pointless—possibly adds to some process that fits into a system of deep and essential consequence.

To know that my actions have little effect on the outcome of national events surely dampens my ego. I am driven to ask why I should make an effort. I begin to question my motives. I wonder why I am driven to work against the overwhelming forces of government. My thoughts wander into strange and sometimes vengeful areas. I begin to hope that things won't go well for our country. I have visions of a government extremely embarrassed by a terrible turn of events. I long for the White House to experience the bitter taste of war's failure. Yet the higher mind wants to be delivered from war and all its terrible afflictions. My mind expands to many polarities. And every direction of my mind's thought lead to some emptiness that must be filled with answers and exquisite reasoning. Perhaps the only answer is to devote myself to helping those who suffer from the impersonality of government, and I would also hope that I receive help when I reach those dark places and can't return by myself.

# February 8, 2003

We went to Royal Gorge today for some cross-country skiing. The snow was very hard and packed down. I was trying out a pair of new backcountry skis. Definitely the snow practice didn't go well with my body: thighs, shoulders, ankles, and wrists seem to be showing the signs of aging.

Psychologically, however, my mind didn't fall victim to the muscular stresses. The snowy silence took me away for just a few hours from the horrible cacophony of city life, TV, news, and the wild journalism caught up in war.

> "Paul, a servant of Jesus Christ, called to an apostle, separated
> unto the gospel of God."
>
> Romans

What does it mean to be "separated unto the gospel of God?" Does the phrase mean that if we are to take a spiritual path, we must separate ourselves from the world? Certainly we exist in the world, but what governs our actions is something other than the drag of politics, power, and materialism.

What does Romans have to do with cross-country skiing? Nothing comes to me specifically, but the idea is to escape to a world covered in snow; a place where the earth is buried under a pristine whiteness. Hence, perhaps the idea of separateness is a symbolic component of the wintry forest. We can glide over the top of all the blemishes below, but at the same time know in our memories what lies beneath. We can deceive ourselves for a few moments and join with natural law, gravity, and the forces connected to bodily motion. Hence, we follow a power greater than us, even if only temporarily. We are separated from our daily world perhaps for only a few hours.

I get the impression that Paul followed a spiritual calling that overtook every part of his life. Is it possible to be like Paul? Could following the steps of Jesus be considered the same as sitting behind a computer for hours, waging war, paying taxes, or watching TV? Are we following a higher power when driving down a crowded freeway? I can easily confuse myself here, unless I decide to focus on the snowy trail and follow it to its end.

# February 10, 2003

We returned yesterday from skiing. President Bush still pressures for war. Laura Bush canceled a few weeks back a poetry reading at the White House. The reason reported was apparently the poets were planning to read antiwar verse. Mrs. Bush felt such political overtones would be inappropriate. Unfortunately the country's poet laureate is antiwar. Interesting how poets have often been persecuted or excluded because their views may not be popular. Ezra Pound, T.S. Eliot, Neruda, and others all found difficulties surviving in their native societies. I had higher hopes for our modern age of openness in so many areas, but the Bush White House seems very intolerant of ideas that might not be popular. I can't imagine that George and Laura would understand the poetic message anyway. I can imagine the threat of moral exposure existed and fear caused Laura's decision.

But today the news stated that Bush will allow just one more week for Iraq's compliance with UN resolutions. This schedule falls in line with Blix's report to the UN, and with some large protests in Washington, San Francisco, Los Angeles, and possibly New York, if the police bend on their current prohibition.

All Muslims will be returning from Mecca. The prayers will be over and bombs can now be dropped without much guilt. At least a few countries seem to be objecting to what appears as complete insanity: France, Germany, and Russia.

The news reports polls that are confusing about what people want in terms of war. I still don't think people understand why the U.S. must go to war with Iraq at this very moment. The childish belief that the President has special information that makes him omniscient still remains ingrained in a majority of American minds.

Rumsfeld said yesterday, "The threat is there to see...Really the only question remaining is: what will we do about it?" Rumsfeld has been chastising France, Germany, and Belgium for not supporting NATO and Turkey in the event Iraq invades this neighboring country. Basically, the U.S. is alienating long time allies because the justification for war is completely unclear. The U.S. leadership—if you want to call it that—is causing these international schisms. The Bush attitude is uncompromising: only one true and just way exists for Iraq and that way is the American way. Therefore, all others who have doubts get out of the way.

I don't feel my concern for war is based on a laisses faire attitude. I believe going to war must be a last resort, especially when an infinite number of peaceful negotiating positions exist. Or, if a country receives an unprovoked attack, then defense may be clearly mandated. We have seen no evidence that Saddam Hussein had anything to do with 9/11, nor is there evidence any active connection exists with al-Qaeda. No, Mr. Rumsfeld, the evidence is not there. Your problem is based on a mind that's quick to abuse and seek revenge.

# February 11, 2003

Please vote for H. Con Res. 2., which repeals Public Law 107-243, Iraq Resolution of 2002. President Bush should not be able to prosecute a war with Iraq without completely justifying the basis before the UN and pursuing inspections to their fullest degree. Please note the serious unraveling of NATO and the UN due to the reticence Germany, France, and Belgium have to a war with Iraq. Please note the extreme accusatory behavior of Secretary Rumsfeld and President Bush as NATO decided not to defend Turkey. The Administration is putting in jeopardy over 50 years of effort to bring governance to international affairs.

> Fred Rounds
> Letter to Congresswoman
> Anna Eshoo
> February 10, 2003

I sent the above letter to my congressional representative yesterday. There isn't a chance in hell that Congress would enact the repeal. It will never get out of committee.

France is receiving heavy criticism for blocking a NATO agreement designed to protect Turkey in the event of an Iraqi invasion. Of course, why is Turkey now afraid when she wasn't before Bush started making appeals for war? France merely wants to be more cautious and she is looking for more evidence that Iraq is a threat. France has offered more aggressive inspections with military support. I think this is the most reasonable compromise yet.

Bush in his bluster and narrowly focused manner continues to press for war. When will the American people begin to realize that Bush has symptoms that closely resemble delusional behavior? He has an exaggerated sense of mission based on his devout religious perspective. He is acting as if he is an instrument of God.

On the surface Bush appears perfectly normal. But, his mind can easily be caught up in the intelligence morass and the limited range of policies he selects from. Since, we're dealing with personality issues more than political, not many ways exist to change things other than blocking maneuvers as France did and as H. Con. Res. 2 is drafted to do. Bush needs to be disempowered from waging war without clear cause.

The very terrifying thought occurs to me that if Bush proceeds off to war, and our military basically dethrones Saddam, would this "victory" intoxicate us to the point that Bush is re-elected. We could have six more years of constant war fear. Except, the next enemies won't necessarily be so weak: Iran, North Korea. We already know the other "evil" nations are nuclear capable as well as having biochemical capabilities. We could easily deplete our countries treasures to the point that our lives could descend into a Gulag and people will wonder what happened. Terrorism will most assuredly grow ever more virulent. As was the case with Oklahoma, American fanatics could emerge to battle for food, shelter, and energy. al-Qaeda will be just another group lost in the chaos of many groups looking for versions of civil rights.

I find our international situation so unbelievable as we now find ourselves in the clutch of war fever. Getting out seems totally impossible at this point.

# February 12, 2003

"And it doesn't harm in these conditions the interest of Muslims to agree with those of the socialists in fighting against the crusaders, even though we believe the socialists are infidels. For the socialists and the rulers have lost their legitimacy a long time ago, and the socialists are infidels regardless of where they are, whether in Baghdad or in Aden. ... "

Osama Bin Laden

http://www.cnn.com/2003/WORLD/meast/02/11/binladen.
excerpts/index.html

Here and there we're finding the above translation of the latest Bin Laden tape. In the case of MSNBC, the above information appeared in one broadcast, and then disappeared in later news programs. Of course, Colin Powell gave a completely biased and deceptive perspective regarding this tape with respect to a relationship with Saddam. From what actually was said, no relationship seems to exist.

We are systematically being lied to by our administration. The White House has lost all credibility with me regarding the budget and war with Iraq. I've never seen an administration create so much damage and crisis in so short a period of time. Congress must find a way to manage this Presidency. I hope

H. Con. Res. 2 makes it out of committee and receives your vote.

Fred Rounds<br>Letter to Anna Eshoo<br>February 12, 2003

Unfortunately with the latest Osama tape the reach was too far. Osama tells of no relationship with Saddam. He merely calls to the people of Iraq to join his quest to fight the crusaders. Iraq will become the cannon fodder for the terrorist war against the Judeo-Christian world: a source for fanatic martyrs.

So far the only message we can really believe is our own need to deal with terrorism. Attacking Saddam right now diverts us from that course and we can see terrorism actually increasing. The President's war against terrorism is failing as he grandstands against Saddam.

A lot of confusing information/propaganda is descending on us right now. The flood of news can make us question our values and perceptions. For me, the important thing to keep in mind is basically that war is rarely a solution to problems. Preemptive war is never a solution. Defense in the event of unprovoked attack may be justified. Yet Bush has not made a case for war with Iraq. He has tried, but failed to convince the world. He has even alienated NATO allies and the UN.

According to recent polls apparently 60 percent of the American people support going to Iraq even without UN backing. I don't know how the polls get done, but I've never been polled. Apparently the people marching in the streets haven't been polled. I continue to wonder whether the polls are just part of the great propaganda machine that basically can't be trusted.

# February 13, 2003

Dear Secretary Colin Powell:

As a Vietnam Veteran and a person of conscience I cannot agree with the arguments you have presented to the UN and the U.S. Congress. You must see the logical inconsistencies and classic examples of circular reasoning, emotionalism, and general propagandizing. We could investigate almost any country in the world and find almost exactly the same sort of intrigue: Certainly North Korean, Libya, Iran, Vietnam, Yemen, Russia, China, Turkey, the U.S., and so on.

There are so many more pressing issues in the world right now that war with Iraq will only divert us from: Terrorism, North Korea, Nuclear proliferation in Libya and Iran, the weakening of NATO and the UN, the impending failure of reforms in Afghanistan, joblessness in America, and so on. Saddam Hussein is 65 years old. I am not expecting my children's children to ever really know Saddam. Containment and deterrence will work with him.

As an ex-Navy officer, I know what Generals must learn to do--say, "yes sir." There are some cases, however, such as My Lai, that conscience must take precedence. I feel a war with Iraq is one of those cases in which the most prudent and moral direction is to say no. Letting go of Vietnam did not bring disaster to America. Our relation with Vietnam is much better now than it was in 1968, and the dreaded domino theory didn't happen. I can't predict the future, and, yes, the future might become more dangerous because we will not be able to control the proliferation of WMD. But, America does have the greatest ability to help others in the world, to develop imaginative and peaceful solutions to disputes.

Vietnam was a terrorist/guerilla war. Did we learn what the most effective tactic was in this type of environment? Certainly it wasn't slash, bomb, and burn. The little successes that I experienced were the moments of caring, sharing, and giving to the locals. Success was bringing resources to the places of need, such as food and things to enhance local commerce. Success involved negotiation and compromise and a willingness to let go of the need to control local government processes. War will only lead us to more terrorism and failure. Please say no to this war.

Fred Rounds

February 12, 2003

I sent the above letter to Colin Powell via the White House. I understand that thousands of messages go to the President everyday that are only collected into some kind of statistical sort, or are never really read at all. The process of writing is more for me to record my voice in the great clutter of noise. I suppose this long letter could be easily summarized in just one sentence:

"Change your mind about Iraq by saying no to war."

# *February 14, 2003*

Hans Blix reported today that Iraq had made some progress in cooperation, but still more needed to be done. What interested me was Blix's remark regarding Colin Powell presentation of the "facts" last week. Blix said that photographs of trucks being moved around at the declared site could just as easily be interpreted as legitimate transport. The inspector found no evidence of WMD at this same site, even though they visited it three times. Powell's arguments collapse substantially when simple logic and inspection are brought to the table. America is beginning to look like a fool and people with good reputations ( Powell ) are leaving the UN chambers looking like liars.

The U.S. is pushing the system very hard to rush into war. But, the world is demanding time to think. And, when we think about what America is doing, arguments begin to totter. If the proponent for war were anyone else but America, he/she would be thrown out in disgrace.

Most of the world wants a positive and sustaining relationship with America. Therefore, the world is acting very politely and definitely not accusatory or hostile toward the U.S. America, however, comes back and impugns the UN for being ineffective. Perhaps we are saber rattling merely for effect. With the lack of world support for Iraq, I can't believe the U.S. would go ahead.

# February 16, 2003

My wife and I went on a peace march yesterday in San Jose. We tried to make an adventure out of the event by biking to the train station and taking the train down to San Jose. Unfortunately the trains don't run on weekends. We decided to try the bus, which can carry two bicycles on the front.

The bus plan worked well. We were dropped off at Roosevelt Park in San Jose where we met about 3500 other marchers.

Again, as I have experienced before, the antiwar protest made a clear statement: "No war in Iraq." According to the SJ Mercury this morning, over 11.5 million people across the world marched yesterday. Apparently 500,000 people gathered in London, over 2-million in Rome. This preemptive protesting is unprecedented. London had the largest protest in her history.

Tony Blair's reaction was for the most part dismissal. He said that Saddam Hussein had killed twice that number of protestors during his regime.

Condoleezza Rice also noted the importance of continuing pressure against Saddam. Popular pressure has not moved the U.S. or British positions. Why? The UN solidly opposed a war with Iraq, except for the U.S., Great Britain, and Spain. Why?

Of course, as I have said repeatedly, we may never see war unless Saddam blinks and decides to take preemptive actions against the gathering troops. At this point a well placed explosive could kill hundreds of Americans located in Kuwait. I don't understand why al-Qaeda hasn't attacked already. The Americans are sitting ducks right now.

Basically, the U.S. warmongering might have more to do with creating fear than actually moving to war.

But, I wonder how long. How long will I keep notes in this journal? Will this journal cross the bridge from peace to war? Bush continues to say he doesn't want war. He most assuredly could turn the troops around, but he won't. He and his cohorts seem to agree that Saddam must go at all costs. Even if the world rebels and decides that Bush is going too far.

## February 17, 2003

The Bush White House has dismissed the massive protests as being foolish, uninformed, and playing into Saddam's hands. Condoleezza Rice basically declared the massive crowds as uninformed. Apparently we don't understand what an awful guy Saddam is. Senator John McCain thinks the protestors are "foolish." Then the marchers were patronized when Condoleezza Rice said that we have a right to protest.

What happens to the human side of people when they enter the halls of American government? Do elected officials forget that we're still living in a democracy? Do our leaders forget that we have an elected government? Are our elected officials supposed to disregard popular opinion? Why does the name Marie Antoinette keep coming up in my mind? Who is really running this government? Why has Congress been so silent lately? I haven't heard from any of our California members of Congress.

I suppose if I were in Bush's shoes, I would test popular opinion in light of the unprecedented protests and act on what he learns. Nowadays people can submit their opinions electronically and instantaneously.

# February 18, 2003

British Foreign Secretary, Jack Straw, said yesterday that the shear enormity of the protests made going to war with Iraq "very difficult," and "we have to take account of public opinion."

I also noted that the stock market rallied this morning. It's up about 150 points.

The Guardian reported on February 17 that if Britain decides to go to war, then antiwar coalition leaders will attempt to shut Britain down with work strikes, building occupation, and sit-down action. Tony Blair, however, isn't listening to his constituents, even though I've never seen such an incredible display of popular protest.

> "Democracy is a beautiful thing. People are allowed to express their opinion, and I welcome people's right to say what they believe. Evidently some in the world don't view Saddam Hussein as a risk to peace; I respectfully disagree."
>
> George Bush
> NY Times
> 2/18/03

Millions of people can express their opinion, but our elected officials don't need to respond, or in the case of Bush, dismiss the public by disagreeing. Bush spins the protest by saying that some people disagree. He's saying that some people—over one-million people in the U.S. alone—can be dismissed as insufficient to change foreign policy. What level of popular referendum would be sufficient? Ten-million? How about 50-million? The latter number would represent about half the electorate appearing at the 2000 polls. The question I would now ask is how many of the protesters who showed up on

February 15 and 16 have acquaintances that sympathize with the protesters' position but didn't march. Personally I could find ten easily. From relatives and neighbors I could probably find another ten. So, if I equate what I can do with what all the other marchers could also do, I imagine that we could assemble 20-million antiwar sympathizers. From polls we see the potential for 50-million people against an Iraq war. I believe Bush needs to be concerned about reelection. Apparently he's not too worried, or he's got something up his sleeve. I frankly don't have a clue how he could pull himself out of this foreign policy mess without serious damage to his future election chances. I should note that these massive protests are occurring before a war has begun. I've never seen anything like this before.

# February 19, 2003

"You know, the size of protests is like deciding, well, I'm
going to decide policy based upon a focus group."

President Bush
SJ Mercury
2/19/03

A "focus group?" Bush thinks a million protesters are tantamount to a
focus group? This type arrogance is beyond my capacity to comprehend.

The protesters have been very peaceful so far. Many of these concerned
citizens come from Middle America. If I project my feelings on the protesters,
I can say that most of the protesters will remain peaceful. They will go home
and continue their lives. But, I think these peaceful masses will not forget
their anger resulting from feeling unheard. That anger will be expressed in
November, 2004 as we go to vote for President.

"It is a violation of laws of armed conflict to use noncombatants
as a means of shielding potential military targets, even those
people who volunteer for this purpose."

General Richard Meyers
CNN
2/19/03

The question comes up as to who would be complicit if both militaries
know that friendly personnel are in a target area, but these militaries proceed
to bomb anyway.

# February 20, 2003

"It is not a satisfactory solution to continue inspections indefinitely because certain countries are afraid of upholding their responsibility to impose the will of the international community," Mr. Powell said.

http://www.guardian.co.uk/Iraq/Story/0,2763,899193,00.html

Powell is speaking of Germany and France in the above quote. He's basically calling these countries cowards. Unfortunately for Powell, invading Iraq is not the will of the international community.

One of the most fundamental principles of the "laws of war" is the protection of civilians.Common Article 3 of the four 1949 Geneva Conventions (the main body of Humanitarian Law) requires all parties to internal armed conflict to treat humanely those taking no active part in the conflict, or who are no longer taking active part. Common Article 3 also prohibits murder, cruel and degrading treatment, torture, and hostage taking. The Fourth Geneva Convention lays out additional protections for civilians in international conflicts.

The fullest statement of the rules governing the conduct of hostilities in international armed conflict, however, is in Protocol I (1977) Additional to the Geneva Conventions of 1949 which has been ratified by over 150 states. Although the U.S. has not ratified it, the fundamental rules on the protection of civilians are widely considered to be part of international customary law and are therefore binding on all states. The rules categorically prohibit:

- direct attacks against civilians or civilian objects (vehicles, buildings and other materials, structures or locations)

- indiscriminate attacks (attacks which do not attempt to distinguish between military targets and civilians or civilian objects.

- disproportionate attacks (attacks which, although aimed at a legitimate military target, have a disproportionate impact on civilians or civilian objects)

http://www.amnesty.ca/Iraq/Iraq_faq2.htm

The above refers to laws of war that can easily be argued to prohibit against knowingly attacking human shields. Amnesty International clearly states its opinion here:

> The forced placement of civilians around a legitimate military target in an attempt to avoid attack is a violation of international humanitarian law and a war crime. Nonetheless, this does not give license to the attacking force to proceed without taking any precautions.

> The obligation to protect civilians during armed conflict applies to all parties. Just as those launching an attack must distinguish between civilians and combatants – or between civilian and military installations – so must those attempting to defend their position.

> "And by spending enough to win a war, we may not have a war at all."

> President Bush
> Atlanta High School
> 2/19/03

Of course, we've spent a lot of money the country doesn't have, and that money has no other purpose but military. And, if we actually go to war, then the value that gets destroyed is irrecoverable.

In the same speech sited above, Bush says:

> [The United States] "joined by many nations. . .is committed to build a world at peace and bringing a better day."

Bush is arguing for a war in order to build this peaceful world. And, I can't conceive of bombs bringing a better day. I imagine Bush is speaking of sometime in the future. My own guess is that the future will be Bush as a private citizen reaping the benefits of an oil conquest.

While everyone's minds are diverted to Iraq, the U.S. will soon send 3000 troops to the Philippines to help fight terrorism. I doubt strongly if terrorism will diminish much around the world because of this exercise in military power. Perhaps we need another Mark Twain.

# *February 21, 2003*

"I understand exactly why people feel so strongly, but in the end, I have got to make a decision and that's the difference between leadership and commentary.

"I have got to make a decision. If we cannot disarm him peacefully, are we just going to ignore the issue and hope it will go away?"

Mr. Blair added: "Who is it that is responsible for conflict if it comes – us, who have done every single thing we can to resolve this peacefully, or him, who refused to abide by the clearly expressed will of the whole of the international community.

"We cannot avoid it by weakness and we cannot avoid it by going back on what we have already said."

Prime Minister Tony Blair

http://politics.guardian.co.uk/foreignaffairs/ story/0,11538,900298,00.html

Here's my response to Blair:

- Are millions of protesters marching against a war just "commentary?"

- The issue doesn't need to be ignored. Try using imagination for a change. Try discussing the matter with a coalition within the Muslim nations to manage Saddam from within. Negotiate!

- We are all responsible. Right now we are the ones holding the gun. You can always decide to not do something, even though egos might be problematic. The whole international community is not expressing the will to use war to disarm Saddam.

- However, we can avoid war by showing our strength and interest in negotiating peace, rather than bullying a country into disarming. America is a country with a gross amount of WMD trying to disarm another country with a lesser amount of WMD. Why not disarm proportionately together?

The scientist behind Pakistan's nuclear bomb is Ayub Qudeer Khan. He visited North Korea thirteen times to transfer nuclear technology. Pakistan seems to be the worst proliferators of nuclear weapons technology, not Iraq. Read *The Nation*, 3/3/3003, Jonathan Schell.

In the same reference above Schell quotes Condoleezza Rice as saying that if Iraq uses WMD, then the U.S. will respond with national obliteration.

Schell also quotes Bush:

> "America has, and intends to keep, military strengths beyond challenge. . .limiting rivalries to trade and other pursuits of peace."

No wonder 83 percent [Time Magazine European poll] of Europeans fear the U.S. more than North Korea or Iraq.

> "The price demanded of us for freedom from the danger of weapons of mass destruction is to relinquish our own."
>
> Jonathan Schell


I agree.

# February 22, 2003

Seymour Hersch, an author often published in the New Yorker, appeared last night on the NOW program with Bill Moyers. Mr. Hersch reiterated what Jonathan Schell says in his Nation article regarding Pakistan. But Mr. Hersch also brought into the argument the rather strange military action we undertook in northeastern Afghanistan [Korkum], wherein we allowed around 3000 al-Qaeda, Taliban, and Pakistani intelligence personnel to be evacuated. The Pakistanis performed this evacuation using ten transport planes. The American military was ordered to provide an escape corridor for these supposedly adversarial troops.

This type of warfare seems all too common in the environment of the modern world in which enemies are not clearly demarked. We may end up attacking people who are supposed to be allies. Of course, such diversity in population is all the more reason why an Iraq war would be unwise. The current ally might be tomorrow's enemy. Such became true with Saddam Hussein.

# February 23, 2003

The Pope has appealed to Blair not to go to war against Iraq. But, what difference does that make when England is considerably protestant. Are we supposed to listen to religious leaders, movie stars, protesters, ex-generals, or the small fringe of congresspeople?

I fantasize about being a Captain Nemo, a person with an array of superior weapons, which I could use to extort peace out of the world: to disarm the world using a greater display of power. Clearly, however, even Captain Nemo's power came to destruction and his plan failed.

Perhaps I am cynical to believe that no amount of military power will bring the end of war. We see in the world right now an increased amount of globalization, diversity, and population mixing. I imagine a time will come when we are in closer touch with people all over the world. When we see the effects of our charity and empathy as opposed to our retribution, we will begin to understand the impacts of and feelings about our policies. Then perhaps our actions will be controlled to some degree by conscience.

We are not at war yet. I think Bush wants to go through all the necessary steps with congress and the UN. He wants to "fully vet" the war option. Unfortunately time is working against Bush because a lot of people are now thinking. The people who lived through Viet Nam need more than a presidential sanction to go to war. They need convincing grounds, such as a response to attack, an "imminent threat" as the U.S. Constitution requires.

# February 24, 2003

I'm getting completely burned out on war talk and thinking. I feel that my mind has grown obsessed with this constant political debate. Some of this obsession stems from my own personality, which doesn't feel adequately heard to begin with, and when my voice is essentially dismissed—as Washington has done with the protesters—I am driven to the point of wanting to scream at the top of my lungs.

Occasionally I need to take a break from the war talk. Other things are most assuredly happening in the world. The weather is like spring outside, even though we're one month away from the equinox.

I will achieve the ability to retire from my current job in about one year. I need to think just one day at a time, however, because so many people are losing their jobs. My wife has been threatened that she may lose her job as a teacher. Education funding took a heavy beating due to the terrible condition of the California state budget: $30-billion in debt.

I find myself being overwhelmed by the news. Hence, my thoughts are drifting back to the war. The mouths in Washington are too big for me to deny:

> The Bush administration hawk [Richard Perle] also indicated that after overthrowing Iraqi President Saddam Hussein, Washington might set its sights on Syria's Bashar Al-Assad.
>
> February 23, 2003
>
> http://www.ptd.net/webnews/wed/bv/Qiraq-us-perle.R8:7_DFN.html

Also, Perle was reported above to have said, "No American President can allow a French head of state to set American policy."

Of course, France isn't setting American policy. She is merely expressing disagreement, and she may reject a second UN resolution which will clarify that Iraq is in breach and will face "serious consequences."

> "I've come to the conclusion that the risk of doing nothing far exceeds the risk of working with the world to disarm Saddam Hussein," Mr.

> Bush said. "Saddam Hussein's refusal to comply with the demands of the civilized world is a threat to peace, and it's a threat to stability."

> http:/www.nytimes.com/2003/02/04/international/ worldspecial/24CND-IRAQ.html

What in God's name does the above statement by Bush mean? Is he declaring war here? What does Bush consider as doing nothing? Inspections? Sanctions? UN Resolutions? Threats of war? What does "working with the world" mean? Does he mean that we should negotiate with the UN members to determine the best possible approach? Or, does he mean that he's decided to go it alone with the part of the world that agrees with the U.S. position?

I believe Bush declared war on Iraq today. The message is somewhat subtle. The quote above is the declaration. The UN Resolution 1441 is the reason. The resolution basically says, "Alright, Saddam, you didn't comply with Resolution 1441. Expect bombs to follow."

The U.S. doesn't expect or care whether the UN votes for a second resolution or not. Bush is declaring the talk over. The next time we hear about Iraq will be after the first raid begins.

# *February 25, 2003*

I convinced myself yesterday that we're going to war. This second UN resolution is just a smoke screen of sorts. Through bribes and other threats directed toward the poorer African countries, such as Angola and Cameroon, we should be able to squeeze out about eleven votes from the Security Council. Only nine are required. Of course, a country like China, France, or Russia could veto the resolution, but such an act would be unlikely because of the divisiveness that would result. Abstention is more likely.

Personally I'd like to see the U.S. vetoed just for the record. My expectation would be that a veto still wouldn't prevent a war. At this point nothing will prevent the U.S. from attacking. No country or collection of countries seems able to stand up to the U.S. style of aggression. We apparently want the Gulf under our control because the region is the energy pivot of the world. Armies are fueled with oil.

I can't think of anything more repugnant right now than an American preemptive invasion of another country. I feel Americans are now learning what Germans must have felt during World War II as Hitler began rolling into France, Russia, and Poland. A two-bit demagogue seems to be driving our country into a moral and probably economic depression.

Yesterday the stock market took a 190-point dip, but then went up about 90 points today. The market has been hovering around 8000 for almost a year. It neither goes up or down too much. The market is like trying to salvage a dream that won't move beyond a middle ground between a nightmare and a paradise. I wonder if a correlation exists between Bush's war speeches and the Dow Jones. I wonder if the peace marches affect the Dow Jones.

Basically, I want something to rescue us from the Bush Administration. Who could that be? No one is stepping up to the challenge. We are powerless.

The Congress appears out to lunch. The Supreme Court appears to be in collusion with the Bush White House. The American people are voiceless. The military is completely in support and ready to obey all orders from the Commander in Chief.

Unfortunately no Daniel Ellsberg is stepping out of the Pentagon with incriminating documentation that exposes the fraud in our government. I imagine many are afraid to say no, except the average peace marcher who shouts "no to war," but with little consequence. A million voices are not enough. One-hundred-and-five cities across America passed resolutions urging no war in Iraq. Two states, Hawaii and Maine, passed similar resolutions. All this civil protest has meant nothing. General Franks needs to say no, but he won't. General Meyers, Chairman of the Joint Chiefs, could say no, but he won't.

# February 26, 2003

http://www.reuters.com/newsArticle.jhtml?type=politicsNews&storyID=2285434

I'm looking at the poll information taken from the above source. The article is deceptive in that it gives the impression that the American people are behind Bush's war push. The article says 55 percent approve of the way Bush is handling Iraq, according to ABC/Washington Post. Then the story quotes a Time/CNN poll showing 54 percent of the sample support military action to remove Saddam.

But to complicate matters the article states—four paragraphs down—that a Zogby poll also shows 54 percent support military action to remove Saddam, but this number falls to 43 percent "when respondents were asked if they would support an attack without significant United Nations or international support. . ." Apparently this Zogby poll showed that opposition to war grew to 50 percent when respondents considered the U.S. going to war unilaterally.

Hence, my conclusion is that the polls are slanted. You ask a narrow question, you'll get a narrow answer. A poll only records the yes's and no's, but not the yes-but's, or no-but's. For example, consider the question; do you support military action to remove Saddam Hussein? You can only answer this question on a poll either yes or no without qualification. But, would you want the U.S. to go to war unilaterally? Maybe not.

However, if we ask the question conditionally, such as:

Do you support unilateral military action to remove Saddam Hussein?

The answer to this question seems to get a very different response than the same question asked, except for the word *unilateral*.

Now, how about the following question:

> Would you support unilateral military action to remove
> Saddam Hussein, even though no clear evidence connects
> Iraq with al-Qaeda, or proves that Iraq is proliferating
> weapons of mass destruction to terrorists, or that Iraq still
> retains any significant quantities of illegal weapons?

The polls show a large group of people may support unilateral action. How many would support a war if the basis for military action is questionable?

Clearly the polls are skewed because the respondents' scope of thought is confined only to the question. If the question provides some education, then the response could differ greatly.

The Reuters article provides additional clues that possibly more educated, experienced, and perhaps disenfranchised people are less interested in war. For example, the Pew poll found that college graduates scored 13 points lower than non-graduates in terms of support for a war. Time/CNN found that 40 percent of people over 65 and 34 percent of African Americans support a war.

What I find extremely disturbing is 85 percent of evangelical Christians support the Bush war. I can see the possibility how a religious crusade fits into the national policy as Bush himself is born again and sometimes borders on preaching during his speeches.

# February 27, 2003

"A new regime in Iraq would serve as a dramatic and inspiring example of freedom to other nations of the region," Mr. Bush said.

http://www.nytimes.com/2003/02/26/international/middleeast/26CND-PREXY.html

Let's see now. We've got the Kurds and the Turkomans to the north of Baghdad. The Turks have made no secret about wanting a Kurdish state. The Shias and Sunnis live primarily around Baghdad or south of it. These groups definitely want autonomy, but the Sunnis and Shias have had many conflicts and Saddam himself is a Sunni. Three-quarters of the Iraqi Army, however, is Shia. Hence, if Iraq is left to its own people to resolve a post-Saddam situation, then I would expect considerable conflict. The Kurd, Sunni, and Shias would most certainly battle for turf and nationalistic autonomy.

And, of course, Iran and Turkey have substantial interest in who runs Iraq. Therefore, somehow the arrival of Americans on their great white horses will convert Iraq into a democracy. No precedent exists in the Middle East for democracy. The closest thing to democracy may ironically be Iraq. The Baath Party is socialist, but a parliament exists and periodic elections are held for national office, even though these institutions are only rubber stamps for Saddam.

Democracy I suppose is possible, but imposing it on a hostile population is tantamount to totalitarianism.

# *February 28, 2003*

Here's a letter I received from Senator Feinstein. I do not include her enclosures.

Dear Mr. Rounds:

Thank you for writing me regarding a possible confrontation with Iraq. I appreciate hearing from you on this important issue.

Secretary Powell made an extremely compelling and comprehensive presentation documenting Iraq's material breach with U.N. Resolution 1441. He showed that Iraq has been practicing deceit and evasion in the arms inspections process. He revealed that Iraq is continuing its weapons of mass destruction program. Secretary Powell showed a nexus between Iraq and al-Qaida.

He provided compelling evidence that Iraq is a real threat to its neighbors and possibly to the United States. He also raised serious questions about whether the arms inspections process as currently constituted can work and whether Saddam Hussein ever intended to comply. I agree with Secretary Powell on these points and because of it's importance I am attaching a copy of Secretary Powell's remarks.

Chief Arms Inspector Hans Blix said it was five minutes to midnight. I think it is even closer. It is now necessary for the Security Council to face up to its obligations and compel compliance by Iraq. A united Security Council and a united world must now face Saddam Hussein with the reality of the actions he must take if he is to avoid war.

I understand the seriousness of this issue and I thank you for sharing your views with me. If you should have additional comments or questions regarding this issue please access my website at feinstein.senate.gov, or contact my Washington DC staff at 202-224-3841.

I replied to Senator Feinstein with the following:

Thanks for your email recently regarding your position on war with Iraq. I regret, however, that your arguments have failed to convince me that President Bush's basis for this war is valid. You seem to be in agreement with Colin Powell's presentation to the UN. This surprises me because most of his assertions have been diminished and/or contradicted, even by Blix. And, of course, Bush hasn't presented any evidence beyond platitude, propaganda, and bombast. In addition your position is out of alignment with your constituency in California. I don't think many would argue that the U.S. military could prevail over the Iraqi forces. I think even the Iraqis have no confidence that they will win against America. Saddam says he's ready to die. So, the real issue is the post war Iraq. What will the conqueror do? Consider the mix: Kurds, Turkomans, Sunnis, and Shias. None of these ethnic groups have traditionally gotten along with each other. Somehow the presence of the white shining horse from America is going to create an "inspirational" democracy. Don't you feel this is the ultimate in arrogance. In addition, if we invade without full and unqualified, un-extorted support from the UN, then we'll face more threats of terrorism, Patriot Act II, and just more repression for the world and ourselves.

I urge you to resist this war. I ask you to support removing Bush's Iraq war authority. I hardly think this congressional resolution is the appropriate constitutional declaration of war. And, I am certain that the U.S. does not have the right to enforce UN resolutions unilaterally, or even multilaterally outside the scope of the UN.

As of this writing 117 cities across America have produced resolutions against war in Iraq. San Francisco and Los Angeles are two of those cities. The grass roots effort against this war is enormous and unprecedented for a war that hasn't even begun.

So many other options exist for dealing with Saddam. To name just a few: Natural causes will one day end Saddam's rule. He's 65 years old. Why not wait. Deterrence and containment have worked with Saddam for the last 12 years. He hasn't presented a threat to anyone, including his closest neighbors. Consider the French alternative. Have we looked at possible trade and negotiation for positive value with Iraq. Obviously, France, Germany, and Russia have been doing this for years. The U.S. has been a trade partner with Iraq in the recent past. We supplied a good bit of her WMD.

Obviously, my view is that Bush and his support troupe is trying to trump up a reason to dominate Iraq. When the American people are forced to think about the basis for this war, they aren't buying. We are not being told the real reasons for this war and I believe we've heard every angle from moral to perceived threat. We've got to challenge President Bush to present the truth behind this war. He has failed to do so as of yet. Colin Powell did a good job, but his arguments ultimately collapsed after a modicum of analysis. I think Colin Powell was Bush's best hope. Could the real truth be that control of Iraqi oil allows the U.S. to dominate the markets of China, Japan, and other countries reliant on Iraqi oil? Could we be looking at America as an empire builder?

The quest for Iraq is taking our minds away from many other immediate and serious issues in America: increasing unemployment, slowing economy, corporate malfeasance, hunger, health, education. Look at California. We have the biggest budget shortfall in years and the federal government is doing little or nothing about it. Look at Bush's budget proposal. A tax cut in the midst of increasing debt? Is this krazy or what? And, $95 Billion for a war in Iraq? There'd better be a good reason to dole out this money, when we're about ready to layoff school teachers. I can't imagine that you'd allocate such funding in light of the millions of children in this country who are coming to school hungry and without proper medical attention. The moral bankruptcy here is beyond imagination.

Fred Rounds


I wonder when the American people will realize that the Bush rhetoric is really the ravings of a mad man.

On my travels to San Diego, I noticed that USA Today has a headline that quotes Bush as saying, "we will disarm" Iraq. This statement alludes to a declaration of war, and war looks much closer now. I don't know exactly when, but arguing against it seems less and less fruitful. We are now dealing with the demonic energy of war.

# *March 1, 2003*

Now that I'm in San Diego, I'm having the interesting opportunity experiencing a more conservative flavor of feelings toward the Bush-Iraq program. The San Diego Union Tribune leans well to the Republican-Evangelical-Bush side.

The opinion page has a piece by Ruben Navarette, Jr., of the Dallas Morning News. Basically he decries the French for resisting the Bush war program and for not appreciating the sacrifices Americans made during World Wars II and I. He argues for boycotting all things French from fries to wine. The ironic thing to me is Navarette looks like a French name. I would imagine that he should change it.

Another complicated shift in the Bush plan is that the White House now demands that Iraq both disarm and remove Saddam Hussein. The UN was only focused on disarmament. Now Bush has raised the bar. Hence, mere disarmament seems a moot point. Why should Saddam do anything at this juncture? I imagine if I were in his shoes, I'd either leave or dismiss the weapons inspectors and prepare for war.

War is now virtually assured. Russia has pulled her officials out of Iraq and U.S. Flag burnings have erupted in Egypt, Bahrain, and Yemen. Brady Kiesling, a senior diplomat based in Athens, resigned in protest to Bush policies. The Iraqi Kurds stated that they will resist if the U.S. lets the Turks join the war within Iraqi borders.

Perhaps the most important thing now is to look at myself. What's driving my antiwar obsession? Bush reminds me of the unstoppable bully, which is an old story for me. I felt surrounded by bullies as a child, and I found no way to stop them. I couldn't stop them. No one could stop them. In some cases these people were even rewarded for their soulless cruelty: social Darwinism, I guess.

Noam Chomsky speaks out about the ills of our government. But, this prominent linguist has been largely dismissed as a voice in political life. He asks the fundamental question that if we're going to demand disarmament of others, then why not of ourselves and the rest of the world? But, Chomsky goes on to claim, "this question never gets asked."

So, bullies are hard to resist when the bully has the advantage. Gandhi overcame the bully because of his overwhelming popular support. Right now America is the bully and no one in the world is willing to apply the necessary pressure to stop the gun pointing.

# *March 2, 2003*

I'm waiting for our flight from San Diego to San Jose to leave, and I'm angry. The security guard surprised us when he informed us that our electronic tickets were no longer valid. Of course, we had already waited in a rather long, serpentine line before we found this out. I mean like how hard would it be to let people know about any policy changes before three-hundred people get in line. The guard directed us into another line for the ticket counter. After getting our tickets straightened out, we had to get back into the line for the security check.

I took off every piece of metal except what might be in my shoes. Unfortunately my shoes set off the metal detector. Another security guard directed me to another line for a thorough check of my shoes. Shit, I thought we were in condition yellow.

According to the *San Diego Union*, U.S. jets are now attacking Iraqi missile trucks as they move into position at the Kuwaiti border. Clearly this type of military action is designed to protect an invading army. The war has started. We're witnessing the target softening stage.

The *Union's* Sunday opinion section, *Insight*, was largely focused on military glorification with a full spread about new technology for naval warfare. The newest ship design concept is called the littoral combat ship (LCS). The LCS can accommodate a variety of decks depending on the application: flight, amphibious landings, SEAL insertion. The article quotes Rear Admiral George Worthington: "[LCS's] cost less and put fewer personnel at risk than one guided missile destroyer...recall the sad statistics of the (three) ships that hit mines in the Persian Gulf."

I thought I was pretty tuned-in to the Gulf War statistics, but I don't have a memory of three ships hitting mines. Of course, during the first Bush war, we had a news blackout.

Going to a different town often provides a different perspective. The Bay Area is very anti-war/-Bush. *Insight's* Editor, Robert J. Caldwell, might represent San Diego as he opines about Bush's vision:

> "Bush's ambitious agenda shows he is, appropriately, thinking
> big. A better future for the tormented Middle East need not
> be an impossible dream."

Need I compliment Caldwell by disagreeing with him? Perhaps the answer would be not to tire myself by trying to present a different point of view.

# March 3, 2003

I couldn't help myself. I sent letters to the San Diego Union:
To: Robert Caldwell

> I read your opinion in the Union-Tribune [3/2/2003]. I live
> in the Bay Area, so I found great interest in encountering
> the more pro-Bush/pro-war perspective in the San Diego
> newspaper. I normally read the San Jose Mercury and the
> SF Chronicle. I would say these papers are moderate-Bush/
> antiwar, anti-Bush/antiwar respectively. I lean toward
> the "anti" side of the house myself, so I didn't agree with
> your opinion. I don't think the narrow focus on Iraq is
> "thinking big". We nail Saddam while Libya, Iran, and
> North Korean build the bomb with technology supplied
> by our good friends, Pakistan and Russia. Is this as big as
> Bush can get?

To: Rubin Nazareth

> I read you opinion "In the end, France won't matter". You,
> yourself, may not be French, but your name looks French.
> Are you going to change it? If we are going to protest to
> the level of food, then I suppose all things French should
> be changed. Hitler tried to remove foreign influence in
> his German language by having dictionaries rewritten with
> Germanic words for everything. Unfortunately, some nouns
> became thirty to fifty letters long. This new vocabulary
> became one of the jokes of Third Reich.

My problem with your opinion is that it's an emotional/ prejudicial reaction to an entire country that happens not to agree with our foreign policy. Your syllogism seems to be as follows: If we helped someone in the past, that someone owes us something now. Or, because we helped France during WWII, they owe us now. Do you see how this logic fails just on the surface? But, suppose the French believe they are beholding to us because of WWII. Should they return the favor by doing something that may be illegal, immoral, or even uneconomical?

War may start next Thursday, according to British news. But, if war does start, it will begin with many people asking questions. Turkey voted against staging U.S. troops within her borders. France and Russia still remain opposed. Unfortunately Bush needs to go ahead. He's trapped.

# *March 4, 2003*

"Oderint dum metuant."

> Lucius Accius
> Roman Tragic Poet (170 BCE)

Let them hate so long as they fear.

This ancient phrase seems to be a fitting remark for our current administration, even though Bush's awareness of this mentality surely eludes him.

> "I just disagree that we need to get U.N. permission to protect ourselves," he [Bush] said. "I'll work with the United Nations; we'll try to bring the United Nations along. But my job is to protect the American people. I sincerely disagree with those who suggest that U.S. foreign policy must be confined to the United Nations."

> "There are people in Germany and France that love Americans," Bush said. "So, yes, I see the protests, and I know they're large at times. But I'm not so sure I'd jump to the conclusion that everybody in those parts of the world are anti-American."

> http://www.bayarea.com/mld/mercurynews/news/
> world/5311293.htm

Bush doesn't seem to admit that protecting ourselves from Saddam was never an issue for the past twelve years. We were successfully protecting ourselves. What we weren't doing is protecting ourselves from the rise of terrorism against American targets.

Not everybody is anti-American, but a large majority is anti-war, and consequently anti-Bush.

Robert Caldwell of the *Union-Tribune* sent me the following message:

> Mr. Rounds,
>
> I think you misread or miscontrued the 'thinking big' passage. It referred not just to Iraq but to the region. Tom Friedman of the New York Times has been writing about this theme for several years now.
>
> Cordially,
>
> Bob Caldwell

I sent him the following reply:

> "Bush sees, first, a democratic Iraq arising from the ruin of Saddam's long oppression. Second, Bush envisions the first Arab democracy as a potential role model for the spread of democratic values in an autocratic region. Third, he hopes for a consequent decline in the poisonous politics that breed hatred and terrorism. Fourth, Bush views the prospective allied victory in Iraq as a catalyst for an Israeli-Palestinian peace."

> How does bashing Iraq produce democracy in the midst of Kurds, Shias, Sunnis, and Turkomans? They've been enemies for years. Even the White House (Tom Ridge) has admitted that an Iraq war may cause a rise in terrorism. Do you think some of the poisonous politics might be our own: for example, the supplying of weapons of mass destruction to Iraq in the 1980's? How can invading Iraq help solve the Israeli-Palestinian conflict? The dots don't connect for me at all here. Has Bush provided answers to any of these questions? You're more in touch with the news than I am, so what is Bush's strategy to make victory in Iraq a catalyst for Isreali-Palestinian peace?

All I can do is ask questions because the logic is missing for me. I have the opinion that anyone who supports a war in Iraq must not be asking questions. Those people must be happy with the rhetoric and platitudes, and must not be concerned for the specific reasons for going to war.

Now here's a note I received from Ruben Navarrette:

"Thanks for the note. Glad the piece stirred you. Maybe we'll agree next time."

I would call Ruben's response to my message a conflict-avoidance answer. I recognize that Ruben probably didn't learn much from what I wrote, but I still believe he should clarify the disposition of his name.

# March 5, 2003

"The vote in Turkey fucked things up big time," grumbles one White House aide. "It pushes our timetable back. On the other hand, it might give us a chance to save face."

Secretary of State Colin Powell, fresh from his latest round of meetings with representatives of countries on the Security Council, delivered the bad news to Bush on Monday.

"You will lose, Mr. President," Powell told Bush. "You will lose badly and the United States will be humiliated on the world stage."

http://www.capitolhillblue.com/artman/publish/article_1870.shtml

Some hints are leaking out that Bush's war strategy might be losing momentum. The world is reacting to a round of disappointments that occurred last weekend. Turkey voted against allowing U.S. troops on her soil, and less than nine members on the Security Council appear ready to vote for war. France, Germany, and Russia have affirmed that they would veto another war resolution.

I have no illusion that the world has suddenly become pacifistic. I think the world is largely against the U.S. staging a preemptive war, especially under such a panorama of arrogance and uncertainty. Few want to recognize the U.S. as a conqueror.

With the escalating threat of North Korea, Bush is now talking about the possibility of military action in Asia. Bush refuses to negotiate with Kim Jong IL. He doesn't seem to understand that North Korea's dictator has an aberrant personality. This dictator's call for help is like a screaming baby. Bush reacts to North Korea only with ego. He thinks baring the chest muscles is the only form of negotiation.

> President Roh was at pains to point out that it was up to Kim Jong Il to abandon his nuclear programme. But U.S. officials are exasperated by his eagerness to engage a Government that devotes resources to its million-strong army, but where as many as three million people have died of starvation.
>
> http://www.timesonline.co.uk/article/0,,3-599956,00. html

What's the alternative? Kill more innocent people to stop people from starving? Why not talk and provide food, if that's possible.

Interesting to note how upset Colin Powell is about the Turkish parliamentary vote. Democracy is great, unless it votes against what the Great Father wants.

> A month after the Sept. 11 attacks, President Bush released a list of the world's most-wanted terrorists. There were 22 names on it. Khalid Shaikh Mohammed was No. 22.

And the list wasn't alphabetical.

> http://www.suntimes.com/output/pickett/cst-nws-pickett04.html

Obviously this story of Khalid Shaikh Mohammed has more to it than what the news sources are capable of telling us. The same article reveals the Khalid was the mastermind of 9/11. How the hell can the mastermind be No. 22.

# March 6, 2003

In the midst of the war mongering we can find some intrigue.

> "Shut up, you dog," Ibrahim said, using one of the worst insults possible in the Arab world, where dogs are considered filthy. The prophet Muhammad discouraged the faithful from keeping them as pets.
>
> Ibrahim also called Sabah "little one" and an agent of the United States and Israel. "A curse be on your whiskers," he said, referring to the facial hair that's a badge of honor in the Arab world.
>
> http://www.bayarea.com/mld/mercurynews/news/world/5328643.htm

Ibrahim is the Iraqi foreign aide appointed to negotiate for Saddam Hussein at an Islamic Summit in Doha, Qatar. Sabah is the representative from Kuwait. Needless to say the meeting didn't go well.

Four of the major government space and weapons contractors Boeing, Hughes, Lockheed, and Loral, provide technology to China to help this Asian country with her space program. None of these companies had licenses to sell goods and services to China, especially technology applied to missiles and/or spacecraft. [see: http://www.nytimes.com/2003/03/05/national/05CND-SPACE.html]. These companies were ultimately fined between 13- to 32-million dollars. What these companies made is not provided in the NY Times story. I make the assumption that the profit is a factor of 10 to 100 times the fine. We also need to keep in mind that China has supplied missile technology to North Korea.

For me, the above history is a good example of how large corporations can easily relax their patriotism and national allegiance when money is involved. We understand that these companies produce a large amount of the U.S. arsenal of missiles, weapons, and jets. Their livelihood is government contracts. But, their clientele seems to be spread out globally, and these companies seem to have no regard for how their technology will be used.

Two things:

1. These companies help keep the world on an equal technological plain, so no one can get significantly more powerful than another.

2. These companies are amoral and they have no apparent national sentiment.

Some small group of people makes a lot of money on the backs of the great masses, who must suffer because this technology produces not much more than waste.

The Guardian [http://www.guardian.co.uk/Iraq/Story/0,2763,908426,00.html ] reported that spy satellite photos of Falluja 2 identified a factory designed to produce chemical weapons. The UN team inspected the plant and Hans Blix reported that the factory may need to be destroyed. The article reveals revealed, however, that a UK subsidiary company under Uhde Ltd. actually built the factory for Iraq's chemical weapons program.

And, I received the following note from Robert Caldwell:

Mr. Rounds,

Wish I had more time to discuss all this with you. Perhaps we could chat on the phone sometime. Oh, and it was the Soviet bloc that armed Saddam in the 70s and 80s, with selective help from the French and South Africans. No American weapons were sold to Saddam.

Cordially,

Bob Caldwell

I had to answer:

Here is a credible reference that describes in substantial detail our shipment of biological dual use technology to Iraq:

103d Congress/2d Session, SENATE, "U.S. CHEMICAL AND BIOLOGICAL WARFARE -RELATED DUAL USE EXPORTS TO IRAQ AND THEIR POSSIBLE IMPACT ON THE HEALTH CONSEQUENCES OF THE

PERSIAN GULF WAR," A Report of Chairman Donald
W. Reigle, Jr., and Ranking Member Alfonse D'Amato of
the Committee On Banking, Housing, And Urban Affairs,
with respect to Export Administration, United States Senate
(198-pages), May 25, 1994.

Yes, France, Germany, Russia, Egypt, Italy, and others supplied additional
weaponry. The 72mm chemical rounds recently discovered in Iraq were
supplied by Russia and Italy. The stories just keep coming how the U.S. and
our allies provided Iraq the means to create weapons of mass destruction.

The minute the UN Security Council approaches agreement that Saddam
needs to be disarmed, the U.S. raises the bar by requiring Saddam's deposal.
Does the Bush Administration really not want the UN to achieve agreement?
I heard on the news yesterday that Colin Powell said that if we need to invade
Iraq without UN approval, then the fate of Iraq will be determined by the
U.S. and its allies alone. Does this mean that the U.S., Bulgaria, Britain, and
Spain will take Iraq and its booty for themselves and no one else?

Since France, China, Russia, Japan, and probably others depend on Iraqi
oil in various ways, perhaps these countries should establish an alliance to
threaten the U.S. to call off the dogs, or face invasion to disarm and depose.

> "I don't see it as a permanent rift," said Karsten D. Voigt, the
> German diplomat who coordinates policy toward America.
>
> "The tone," Mr. Voigt said, was that "the Europeans are not
> needed, that they reflect something old and that, at best,
> they are irrelevant."
>
> "Russia is prepared for a kind of compromise," said Vladimir
> P. Lukin, a former ambassador to Washington. "But what
> kind of compromise can you have if the U.S. doesn't want
> to hear anybody?"
>
> http://www.nytimes.com/2003/03/06/international/
> europe/06ASSE.html?pagewanted=2
>
> "We don't need UN approval."

President Bush
News Conference
March 6, 2003

Bush is dividing himself from the rest of the world. He says he doesn't
want war, but he leaves himself few options. He argues with the UN, but
dismisses its authority and mission. He displays a disdain for those countries
who disagree with our policy.

Hans Blix and El Baradei reported today that to date no current WMD program has been found and no evidence exists of a nuclear program. Yes, uncertainty still exists regarding unaccounted-for chemicals and biological agents. Iraq still is not forthcoming with information, but she is definitely not building an invasion force. Iraq seems to be preparing to be invaded.

In the midst of international chaos over our stance with Iraq, Bush is looking more and more foolish, perhaps mentally unstable. Even Saddam is calling an invasion "stupid." As much as I find the idea distasteful, I could almost agree with Saddam.

France, Germany, Russia, and China are literally trying to stop the U.S. from going to war. They are threatening a veto. If this veto actually happens, and we proceed to war, I see no real option but to dismantle the UN and return to the era of suspicion, espionage, and endless conflict. Bush needs to be stopped, but the Congress is just silent. The Supreme Court is totally silent. A large part of our country is outraged, but ineffectual.

The U.S. and UK have come up with a new compromise resolution to give Iraq ten more days to show compliance with Resolution 1441, or disarmament. Of course, I think everyone realizes the unreality of such a resolution. What does compliance mean? Without inspections, how can we ever check for compliance, and what criteria must be used to insure compliance. Every report UNMOVIC has made so far just infuriates the U.S. as just more evidence of Iraq's obstruction. In addition, disarmament means also the removal of Saddam. How could Saddam be removed without the use of military?

I heard Jack Straw say last night that disarmament doesn't mean Saddam needs to go. The U.S. and UK are in disagreement on this point, I guess.

In the mean time, North Korea has tested more missiles and continues to start up its nuclear program. Apparently North Korea presents no problem for the U.S. We can solve this theater of issues with diplomacy by letting Russia, China, South Korea, and Japan work out the details. Bush calls North Korea a "regional problem." What in God's name is going on with Bush? I feel like a character in Tolstoy's *War and Peace.*

# March 8, 2003

The U.S. and UK have put a resolution before the UN giving Iraq ten days to disarm, or else. March 17 will be the day of reckoning whether Iraq will be in compliance. Of course, the resolution provides no guidelines as to what compliance means, or any sort of measure that could be used by anyone that would demonstrate that disarmament has or will be completed. What if Iraq really doesn't have any WMD left, and she doesn't have complete records of disposal. How does anyone determine whether Iraq is lying or not? The resolution is a farce. The U.S. and its allies know that further resolutions to sanction war will not work. I think the U.S. wants to just say she tried, even while knowing that most sane governments would disapprove.

The U.S. and UK have tried reasoning, but the reasoning continually falls short of fact. Today the *NY Times* reported that Mohamed EL Baradei, chief IAEA, said that Iraq's attempt to buy uranium yellow cake from Niger was untrue. British intelligence apparently reported that such attempted imports had occurred. However, these intelligence reports were based on fake documents.

http://www.nytimes.com/2003/03/08/international/
middleeast

Why does the U.S. and UK continually put flawed information before an international body of experts? We are being made fools of.

I also don't understand why the Security Council doesn't put forward a resolution directing the U.S., UK, Spain, Bulgaria to back off. Why doesn't our Congress ask Bush to back off? I see Bush trapped into going to war, even if he doesn't really want to. I see so much risk for both the U.S. and Iraq. The U.S. has such a volume of troops and weapons to move into Iraq that we are left open to devastating surprise and guerilla attacks. I hope we are prepared.

Gasoline prices are going up right now. Regular is close to two dollars per gallon. I also noted that defense contracts for fuel were awarded to a long list of oil and gas companies. The following is a partial list:

| | |
|---|---|
| Shell Oil | $323,163,680 |
| Conoco Phillips | $105,001,855 |
| Air British Petroleum | $97,599,950 |
| Coastal Aruba Refining | $95,520,745 |
| Citgo Petroleum Corp. | $80,011,103 |
| Valero Marketing and Supply | $54,952,814 |
| Garry-Williams Energy Corp. | $51,950,241 |
| Age Refining | $39,769,380 |
| Premcor Refining | $32,072,837 |
| Tesoro Refining | $20,110,489 |
| Alon USA | $19,915,700 |
| Hermes Consolidated | $18,230,226, |
| Western Petroleum | $17,214,400 |
| Conoco Phillips [again] | $14,622,922 |
| Exxon Mobil | $389,947,257 |
| Placid Refining | $57,261,780 |
| Pride Companies | $17,612,857 |

http://www.defenselink.mil/news

These awards were made on two separate days during March, 2003. Of course, these procurements could be completely normal for the daily operation of the military. About half of these companies are either from or scheduled to do business in Texas, Bush's home state. Yet, much of the oil business exists in Texas. Also of interest is that Bush owns or he has previously owned stock in Exxon Mobil. This company received the largest contract award.

Could this defense demand for fuel be forcing prices up for the general populace? If we translate these numbers into gasoline prices at the pump, we would be able to fuel 25-million cars for a week using my gasoline consumption as a model. When I look at these numbers—a billion or so dollars—I don't see anything inordinate, except perhaps the desire to find something about Bush that would trash his presidency.

I should note that Exxon Mobil was one of Bush's largest campaign financiers.

# March 9, 2003

George Bush pulled out of a speech to the European Parliament
when MEP's wouldn't guarantee a standing ovation.

A source close to negotiations said last night: "President Bush
agreed to a speech but insisted he get a standing ovation like
at the State of the Union address.

http://www.mirror.co.uk/news/allnews

I imagine that an unelected president needs to surround him/herself
with agreement so as not to convince people of their good judgment in not
electing him/her.

"We are in self-preservation mode right now," Capt. Jeff
Beirlein said. Soldiers serving as guards got lost walking
their posts.

http://www.nytimes.com/2003/03/08/international/
middleeast

Apparently 17 tents blew down in a fierce sandstorm in Kuwait. Soldiers
were exposed to the elements, and unable to fight. I suppose if the military
is left sitting in the desert, the opponents won't need to do anything because
nature will do all her work. The loss of 17 tents implies that almost 1000
soldiers had their shelters blown away.

According to the Sunday Herald, ten non-permanent members of
the Security Council, the Vatican, and some "moderate" Arab states have
proposed adding a directive to the second resolution for UN adoption. This

proposal gives Saddam 72 hours to put himself and his family into exile. If he doesn't accept this resolution, then expect war. Will this resolution see the light of day? We may know something this Tuesday. I still don't like the idea of going to war for the reasons we've been given so far.

Jimmy Carter wrote an opinion for the *New York Times* today. He flatly opposes a war with Iraq because such an action is unjustified based on all that Bush has said so far.

# *March 10, 2003*

In an ominous warning for his son, Mr. Bush Sr. said that he would have been able to achieve nothing if he had jeopardized future relations by ignoring the UN. "The Madrid conference would never have happened if the international coalition that fought together in Desert Storm had exceeded the UN mandate and gone on its own into Baghdad after Saddam and his forces."

http://www.timesonlilne.co.uk/article/0,,3-605441,00.html
I wonder how closely G.W. listens to his Father. I'm also amazed that few, if any, U.S. newspapers carried the above story.

"If there is a resolution passed and he hasn't done what is required by the 17th, then he's lost his chance," said Powell, referring to Saddam. "At that point, I think there's a high likelihood that military force is what's going to disarm Saddam Hussein by changing his regime."

http://www.bayarea.com/mld/mercurynews/5356997.htm
What is Saddam required to do?

Apparently three Iraqi soldiers already surrendered at the Kuwaiti border because they thought the war had begun. The U.S. forces informed these men that war hadn't begun. The U.S. military then sent the confused men back to wherever they came from. These soldiers appeared to be in terrible shape. Unfortunately we sent them home. Just think of the fabulous opportunity we had. We could have capitalized on the image of the Iraqi army deserting before even a shot is fired.

# March 11, 2003

The cafeteria menus in the three House office buildings will change the name of "French fries" to "freedom fries," a culinary rebuke of France, stemming from anger over the country's refusal to support the U.S. Position of Iraq.

www.cnn.com
3/11/03

The French bashing I find very disturbing. I happened to read an editorial by Rubin Navarrette Jr. of the Dallas Morning News in which he says:

> "Now Americans should register their disgust. And the best way for them to do so is to snap shut their pocketbooks. You've heard the stories of outraged American restaurateurs canceling orders for French wine to show their patriotism....
>
> That's a good start..."

The following is an email I sent to Mr. Navarrette—a man with a French name.

> Ruben,
>
> There's some people that might agree with your perspective on things French. I personally find situations such as these [displays of ethnic bias] frightening. I need to believe that our leadership in Washington is evaluating current events in light of facts. What can you

do to help prevent the anti-French fervor from getting out of hand?

Thanks,
Fred

Then along with Congress-people throwing French wine down the sewer, illegal weapons evidence starts to crumble.

> "These documents—which formed the basis for the reports of recent uranium transactions between Iraq and Niger—are in fact not authentic," ElBaradei told the United Nations on Friday.

> "With respect to the uranium, it was the information that we had," Powell said. "We provided it. If that information is inaccurate, fine."

> http://abcnews.go.com/section/GMA/2020/
> GMA030310Iraq_weapons_evidence.html

So, providing false information to the world in order to rally support for a war is "fine"? How can we believe anybody in the White House right now, if our leaders have such a cavalier attitude about the truth?

Another U.S. Foreign Service diplomat resigned because he disagrees with the Bush policy on war with Iraq. His name is John Brown.

> "The president's disregard for views in other nations, borne out by his neglect of public diplomacy, is giving birth to an anti-American century," he said.

> http://www.smh.com.au/articles/2003/03/11/1047144951
> 200.html

Then we have the bombs to scare everyone.

> The Air Force on Tuesday tested for the first time the biggest conventional weapon in the U.S. military's arsenal, a 21,000-pound munition that could play a dramatic role in an attack on Iraq.

> http://www.nytimes.com

Some suggestion exists that we shall use this bomb in our attack on Iraq. I keep in mind that a weapon of this magnitude would be considered a weapon of mass destruction. The look and feels of these conventional weapons are approaching the nuclear technology used on Hiroshima. Of course, we bring into play the threat of these large weapons while we don't rule out the possibility of going nuclear as well.

# March 12, 2003

Hints are appearing that some Iraqi generals are negotiating a possible surrender before even the first shots are fired. I realize that surrender would be superior to war. Such an approach would display the wisdom of all. But, I would hate to see Bush become a hero out of this tragic set of circumstances.

The British and U.S. are still trying to push the boulder uphill and get UN sanction for the war. So far the conditions are as follows:

- A television appearance by Iraqi President Saddam Hussein renouncing weapons of mass destruction.

- Iraq's permitting 30 key weapons scientists to travel to Cyprus to be interviewed by U.N. weapons inspectors.

- Destruction "forthwith" of 10,000 liters of anthrax and other chemical and biological weapons Iraq is allegedly holding.

- Surrender of and explanation about biological weapons production.

- Commitment to destroy proscribed missiles.

- Accounting for unmanned aerial vehicles.

http://www.cbsnews.com/stories/2003/02/24/iraq/main541815.shtml

One of the unmanned aerial vehicles turned out to be made of balsawood and duct tape. It was powered by what looked like two weed whacker motors. The particular flying model had a 24.5-foot wingspan. Colin Powell mentioned that we should be deeply concerned because this drone could be equipped to spread germs and toxic chemicals. Colin Powell may be right, but he's stating his opinion. The drones could be used for other things: surveillance, aerial photography, mapping, and flight research.

With all the intelligence failures to date, we really don't know how much Anthrax is still in Iraq. So, 10,000 liters of poison might be hard to come up with.

The list above, however, seems very small in light of the hoopla stirred up by the U.S. and UK. I note that Saddam is not asked to step down. Apparently if Saddam does all the things on the list, he will remain in power and sanctions will be lifted. Saddam has repeatedly said publicly that Iraq has no WMD. The Al Samoud missiles are being destroyed right now.

The remaining items on the list seem arbitrary, and probably these tasks could be accomplished in a day or two. Clearly the British—the principle authors of the list—are looking for a face-saving way out of going to war. The U.S. also seems to be going along with the British proposal. Could we be looking for a way out of this impending war? Could Daddy Bush have gotten through to his son?

# March 13, 2003

The threat of war drags on. Any UN resolution has been delayed until maybe next week. From the American perspective a UN no vote means we go to war without UN sanction. A yes vote means we go to war, if Iraq doesn't comply with UN resolutions by a certain date. We can be very suspicious that Iraq will not or simply cannot comply no matter how well intentioned.

Yet, the behavior of the U.S. and UK is so unusual that I wouldn't be surprised if we didn't go to war at all.

These drone planes continue to turn out to be short range experimental models cobbled together with aluminum foil, duct tape, and salvaged parts. To think that they could be used in a combat environment is ludicrous. They wouldn't last in the sky long enough to disseminate much of a weapon. The U.S. seems to be acting on paranoia.

> "He made the reason for this as the fact that the French have become completely intransigent and literally threatened to veto anything that is put forward to the U.N. Security Council," the Tory leader said.
>
> http://www.nytimes.com/2003/03/13/interatiional/europe/13CND-BRIT.html

The Tory leader mentioned above is Iain Duncan Smith. He's complaining about the French who have continually threatened to veto any resolution that leads to war automatically. What we see is an evaluative observation on the part of Duncan that generally has led to some French-U.S.-UK aggravation. I'm getting a sense, however, that Tony Blair would like to forget the day he ever agreed to partner with the U.S. regarding a war with Iraq.

# March 14, 2003

Because Bush merely mentioned 9/11 and Saddam Hussein in the same breath during a number of his speeches, around 45 percent of the American public—according to a CBS poll—believe Saddam was involved. Bush has never provided evidence or accused Saddam of any relationship to 9/11, nor has the FBI, CIA, or any other credible source provided any evidence. None of the hijackers were Iraqi.

Obviously people don't need much information to drive them to conclusions. I suspect people in high office become acutely aware of human gullibility, and I am also sure that communications experts are constantly feeding the President carefully crafted information to help the listeners make a politically desired—not necessarily logical—conclusion. Of course, propaganda is designed to sway opinion.

> Tony Blair's problems over Iraq deepened yesterday when Robin Cook, the Leader of the Commons, suggested he would resign from the Cabinet if Britain went to war without a clear United Nations mandate.
>
> http://news.independent.co.uk/politics/story.jsp?story=386919

Yeah, well, so what? Until some nonexpendable drops out, the war will go on. And, yet, who really is nonexpendable?

> "But we don't have that much time," a State Department official said. "It's not because warmongers are ready to march. It's because it would be self-defeating to let Iraq off

the hook by even two or three weeks, when you know they will just squirm out of their obligations again."

"Diplomacy is slipping away, and Rumsfeld needs some duct tape put over his mouth, but Powell is not coming unglued," a friend of the secretary said. "He's comfortable with the policy of using force as a last resort."

http://www.nytmes.com/2003/03/14/international/middleeast/14POWE.html

Who is the "they" that's squirming out of obligations? I can imagine that the "they" is only Saddam himself and those that choose to follow him. So, if Saddam is removed from office, the squirming would end. Unfortunately the State Department official doesn't communicate the specifics and the American people may be left thinking that all Iraqis are squirming.

Apparently a friend of Powell's believes that Rumsfeld is a warmonger. Yet, Powell still is pushing hard for war. So, from the outside Rumsfeld and Powell look about the same.

"The plan includes simultaneous ground invasions from north and south... It also includes a sudden decimation of Baghdad by raining down on its people, in two days, over 800 cruise missiles -- more than were used in the entire Gulf War. Ullman... characterized the Baghdad assault thusly: 'You have this simultaneous effect, rather like the nuclear weapons of Hiroshima, not taking days or weeks but minutes.' It would be a firestorm, a Dresden or Tokyo with 60 years of new technology. It would be a war crime of quick and staggering proportions."

http://www.zmag.org/content/showarticle.cfm?SectionID=51&ItemID=3119

No sense in arguing the validity of what will happen at the beginning of hostile action. The propaganda that comes out beforehand is meant to scare. Whatever happens, the results will be ghastly and most assuredly criminal.

In 1995, General Kamel was debriefed by senior officials of the United Nations inspections team, then known as UNSCOM, and by the International Atomic Energy Agency. The complete transcript, now disclosed for the first time, contradicts almost everything Bush and Blair have said about the threat of Iraqi weapons.

> For example, General Kamel says categorically: "I ordered destruction of all chemical weapons. All weapons - biological, chemical, missile, nuclear - were destroyed." All that remains, he says, are the blueprints, computer disks and microfiches.

> http://www.zmag.org/content/showarticle.cfm?SectionID= 51&ItemID=3235

I'd like to think the information above is true, but we have found Al Samoud missiles. However, Newsweek thought the Kamel story was true enough to report it on February 24, 2003. The complete debriefing of General Kamel can be read at:

> www.fair.org/press-release/Kamel.pdf

Kamel does admit to destroying chemical and biological weapons in this transcript. Yet, the CIA has denied the documents veracity. I would like to stay with facts, but knowing the best possible truth seems about as tenable as grasping fog.

# March 15, 2003

"The chemical attack on Halabja, just one of 40 targeted at Iraq's own people, provided a glimpse of crimes Saddam Hussein is willing to commit, and the kind of threat he now presents to the entire world. He is among history's cruelest dictators, and he is arming himself with the world's most terrible weapons," Bush said.

Bush went on to quote Nobel laureate and Holocaust survivor Elie Wiesel as saying: "We have a moral obligation to intervene where evil is in control. Today, that place is Iraq."

http://www.reuters.com/newsArticle.jhtml?type=politicsNews&storyID=2385510

The objective of Bush's comments is to make people afraid. If Bush wants to see cruelty, just watch the show from the ground up when our bombs and troops start rolling in.

Frankly this cruel dictator, Saddam, isn't taking advantage of the military situation when our troops are most vulnerable, particularly during sandstorms and such. The troops are congregated in a small area just across the border. A few well-placed bombs and American would have a tragedy to deal with. Of course, the U.S. response would be immediate retaliation and off we would go to war. But, Saddam likely won't start anything for two big reasons:

1. U.S. troops are in Kuwait. So, a preemptive strike would be an invasion of another country.

2. Saddam knows the U.S. would retaliate with an overwhelming force.

If Saddam were a better military strategist—he's actually one of the world's worst along with being cruel—he would try to string the U.S. troops along for an extended period of time: hit and run tactics, sabotage, guerilla warfare.

# March 16, 2003

I just heard Blair and Bush speak at the Azore Summit. They've decided to give the UN one more day, tomorrow, to come up with a resolution regarding Iraq. Personally, this ultimatum spells the end in my view. The U.S. along with a paltry few will invade Iraq. The U.S. now becomes a pariah in the world.

The disclosures came as the ranking Democrat on the Senate Intelligence Committee called for the FBI to investigate.

> The documents "may be part of a larger deception campaign aimed at manipulating public and foreign policy regarding Iraq," Sen. John D. "Jay" Rockefeller IV (W. Va.) said in a letter to the bureau.

> http://www.latimes.com/la-fg-docs15mar15,0,5016930.story

Of course, the Bush Administration has been pressuring the CIA to come up with evidence, but whether the intelligence is true or not seems completely immaterial.

> A small group composed mostly of retired CIA officers is appealing to colleagues still inside to go public with any evidence the Bush administration is slanting intelligence to support its case for war with Iraq.

> Members of the group contend the Bush administration has released information on Iraq that meets only its ends – while ignoring or withholding contrary reporting.

http://www.kansascity.com/mld/kansascity/news/breaking_
news/5393854.htm

*Oh, play spy somewhere else, you old gas bags.* Such is the attitude of the
new CIA.

Oil giants BP and Shell were among a group of 15 British
companies which met with government officials this week to
lobby for lucrative reconstruction work in Iraq.

http://www.thescotsman.co.uk/business.
cfm?id=312762003

The vultures are already circling.

President Bush said Sunday the opportunity for a diplomatic
solution to the confrontation with Iraq would end Monday,
calling it "a moment of truth for the world."

http://www.cnn.com/2003/WORLD/meast/03/16/sprj.irq.
main/index.html

Bush's may be declaring his only moment of truth as he decides to bash
Saddam.

Bush has opened the jaws of war and the lemmings are rushing in.
Nothing is stopping the President: not the protests, not the Congress, not the
UN, not the courts, not previous Presidents including Bush, Sr. I keep asking
how could this insane series of events be happening? How could a nation
based on democracy buy into a preemptive war?

# March 17, 2003

Bush, in a televised speech set for 8 p.m. ET, will demand that Saddam yield power and leave the country, the White House said.

"Obviously we seem to be at the end of the road," Annan said at the U.N. news conference.

http://www.cnn.com/2003/WORLD/meast/03/17/sprj.irq.main/index.html

We're at the end. No new resolution will be put before the UN today. The President will speak tonight to give Saddam an ultimatum: leave in 72 hours or face war.

My predictions:

1) A lot of Iraqi troops will surrender without a fight.

2) We'll never see Saddam again.

3) No WMD will be found or used because Saddam has none.

The months of provocation and accusation about WMD will turn out to be much ado about nothing.

Robin Cook, the British government's highly respected leader in parliament and a former foreign secretary, resigned on Monday in protest at Prime Minister Tony Blair's hawkish stance on Iraq.

http://www.reuters.com

Some integrity remains.

Lord Goldsmith, the British Attorney General, says that war with Iraq is legal and sanctioned by Resolutions 678, 687, and 1441. Apparently these resolutions authorized removing Iraq's WMD by force if Saddam decided not to remove them. I disagree with Lord Goldsmith because the resolutions belong to the UN and must be enforced by the UN. The U.S., UK, and Spain are planning to invade Iraq as agents independent of the UN. I would say that such an invasion would not be legal from the UN viewpoint. But, who cares? Our unfettered President has decided to start killing people.

> I believe one of your prerequisites for going to war with Iraq is UN approval. President Bush does not have UN approval for the U.S., UK, and Spain to invade Iraq. We are planning to invade Iraq independently. President Bush is going to start killing people. I wager that very few people, if any, could give a cogent reason for invading Iraq. We might be able to regurgitate what we hear on TV, but we haven't been told much of anything that holds up under scrutiny. Consider the trumped-up Iraq-Niger uranium deal. The documents were faked. Consider Powell's presentation to the UN. Every piece of evidence Gen. Powell presented is wrong, out-of-date, or open to wide interpretation. We claim to know that Saddam has WMD, so we provided some of our intelligence to the inspection team. The inspection team has visited the suspected sites multiple times and has found nothing to date. Now the inspectors have been ordered to leave, so we shall never know who is telling the truth. We tried and failed to establish a clear connection between Saddam and al-Qaida. The President continues to say that Saddam has had twelve years to comply with UN resolutions. But, during those twelve years Saddam hasn't used WMD, nor do we know for certain that he has resurrected his ability to produce WMD. The reasons for a war now seem very flimsy. I do not understand the administration's motives. I can only presume that the administration's anxious press for war arises out of serious and dangerous instabilities in the minds of our leaders. I urge strongly that we call an emergency session of Congress to question the reasons for this war.

Today I sent the above message to Senators Boxer and Feinstein. I believe Bush should answer a severe set of questions before going off to war. Yet, Congress doesn't seem to be asking those questions.

Jack Straw said: "Over the months since resolution 1441 was unanimously adopted by the security council in early November, my right honourable friend the prime minister and I and our ambassador to the United Nations have strained every nerve in search of that consensus which could finally persuade Iraq by peaceful means to provide the full and immediate cooperation demanded by the security council."

http://www.guardian.co.uk/Iraq/Story/0,2763,916286,00.html

The "strain," of course, was the resistance the UN produced against the idea of war as the only option to resolving the WMD issues with Iraq. Only three countries on the UN Security Council joined in a war option: U.S., Spain, and the UK.

I'm listening to Bush give Saddam a 48-hour ultimatum: leave or face war. I thought we were considering a 72-hour warning.

# March 18, 2003

The hours leading up to the debate saw two more ministers resign, John Denham from the Home Office and Lord Hunt from the Health Department, following robin Cook's departure from the Cabinet yesterday, and the resignation of four Parliamentary Private Secretaries, ministerial aides.

http://www.thisislondon.com/news/articles

The U.S. has had only two notable diplomats leave office due to Bush's foreign policy. America seems to be now in a frenzy of war support. Even Pelosi and Feinstein are "getting behind the troops." No outrage comes from our leadership who oppose this war. No effort is being made to protect our troops by bringing them home.

Recent inspection teams have included a new batch of U.S. nuclear scientists from Lawrence Livermore and Los Alamos national laboratories. The U.N. official described these inspectors as arriving as hawks and leaving as doves, after finding Iraq, "a ruined country, not a threat to anyone." It is a view radically different than the administration's.

http://ww.bayarea.do/mld/mercurynews/5418901.htm

The only resistance we shall have is Saddam's resistance. He refuses to capitulate. What else is new? Kofi Annan has removed all UN personnel from Iraq, and he has stopped the oil-for-food program. Without relief soon 70% of the Iraq people will either starve, or have difficulty getting enough food. Relief will only come after we invade.

Saddam doesn't appear to be putting significant amounts of military equipment and personnel at strategic locations. Iraq hasn't taken any offensive measures beyond fortifying Baghdad to some degree. Apparently U.S. intelligence believes that Iraq is supplying some troops with chemical weapons. Of course, such usage would confirm the accusations from the Bush Administration. If the U.S. doesn't find anything, then Bush will have lost all credibility. I'm hoping we don't find anything. I don't want Bush to have anything easy over making this decision.

My wife got a pink slip yesterday. This notice is more fallout from a failing economy and budgets being diverted to defense and security. My wife is a teacher who gives her time to help many people learn to read. Her program is being severely cut. More people will move into ignorance and cultural disability because of weakness in reading skills.

> The United States Congress has stepped in to find nearly $300m in humanitarian and reconstruction funds for Afghanistan after the Bush administration failed to request any money in the latest budget.

http://news.bbc.co.uk/2/south_asia/27559789.stm

I imagine Afghanistan will return to her major product: heroin.

Perhaps thirty countries will support the Iraq war, but none of the thirty are Canada, Mexico, Russia, China, France, and Germany. Canada helped during Afghanistan, but does not see the reason to help in Iraq. France is being singled out as the wrench in the machine, even though Russia and China threatened veto.

Why wouldn't Iraq prepare her weapons and troops to oppose an invasion? My opinion is Saddam may be preparing for different kind of resistance than before. I'm thinking about guerilla style warfare. If he spreads his troops out widely, Iraq would be less vulnerable to bombing and the soldiers would be more available to hit and run.

Saddam could also exile himself anytime. The man is unpredictable. He's a terrible military tactician because his ego gets in the way. He could probably defeat any invasion force by capitalizing upon the natural features of Iraq: desert, swamps, heat, and rugged territory. His mind moves to old style land battles with huge armies facing off with each other. This kind of warfare became obsolete during the Civil War.

Theoretically Saddam should have significant advantage over an invading force. He could get the U.S. forces stuck in any number of quagmires. Perhaps combatants from both sides are fortunate that Saddam is so incompetent. The loss of life will be low and surrender will be high. I would recommend

Saddam read Ho Chi Minh and Mao Tse Tung. We haven't been able to overcome their style of guerrilla warfare.

By a vote of 412 to 149 the British Parliament supported Blair in his Iraq policy. The U.S. Congress will not vote again. Saddam Hussein has made his intentions clear. He will not step down. I sent the following letter to Diane Feinstein:

> The Congress now is rallying around the troops. We are all hoping for the best outcome. However, I vehemently disagree with the President on his bulldozing into Iraq. I definitely do not support his policies and I feel sorry for the troops that must become the instrument of foreign conduct. I understand this terrible assignment because I'm a Vietnam War veteran who was and remains very conflicted regarding my military duties. The best thing for our troops is to bring them back home.
>
> Congress has the responsibility to declare war. Congress is also the check and balance for the President. The President doesn't have the political competence to analyze and comprehend the complexities of foreign politics. He's incapable of answering tough questions, such as how does he justify legally going-it-alone against Iraq, when Kofi Annan says such an act falls outside the UN Charter? Or, since the inspectors have yet to find any WMD, and since American IAEA inspectors are saying that Iraq is "a ruined country, not a threat to anyone," why are we hell bent to occupy this country? Now we are standing by and allowing a person of questionable mental stability to send American youth to possibly die and most assuredly kill. I agree with Tom Daschle. The President's diplomacy has been a joke. To give it any sort of credence would be too complimentary. We can't be political when people are about to die. We need to feel sure that going to war is absolutely the right thing to do.
>
> I feel very sure that we have not heard any convincing argument that war is a better approach for Iraq than continuing to work with the UN inspection team and humanitarian agencies.
>
> Please support our troops by saving their lives and condemn the administration for their disturbed, narrow, and dangerous view of the world. You may be in the minority now, but most

of the time wars never produce the desired end product. Look at the history: This is the second Gulf war; Afghanistan has returned to being the heroine capital of the world; we're still struggling to democratize Kosovo; Vietnam returned to some degree of stability only after we left; we're still fighting the Korean War; Somolia was a disaster, and so on, and so on. History would probably erase any ill will that would crop up now because you took a stance against the President.

Please speak out and try to save our soldiers and the innocent people of Iraq. The State Department's top counterterrorism official said Tuesday there is a "certainty" terrorists will try to "launch multiple attacks" and a senior intelligence official told CNN there is "a near certainty of small scale al-Qaida attacks" against U.S. targets.

http://www.cnn.com/2003/US/03/18/sprj.irq.terror.alert/index.html

O.K., we have the report. Now tell me when. Ever since 9/11 the Administration has sent out alerts, but so far nothing has happened. I would say that a better approach would be to live in fear rather than continually promulgate hysteria.

# March 19, 2003

Though I appreciate what Congressperson Eshoo has tried to do, clearly Bush is much like Saddam Hussein. He needs a very loud signal for him to react. The threat of impeachment may be the only action he understands.

> A UN weapons inspector who returned from Iraq yesterday said today that the U.S. had given them wrong and misleading information about Iraq's weapons of mass destruction.
>
> Jorn Siljeholm, 48, a Norwegian scientist at the Massachusetts Institute of Technology, spent 100 days in Iraq as part of the UN inspections team.
>
> He told the Associated Press that assertions by U.S. officials, including the U.S. secretary of state, Colin Powell, about Iraq's arsenal and its attempts to hide it, did not tally with his own findings.
>
> "None of their hot tips were ever confirmed," he said, adding: "I don't know about a single decontamination truck that didn't turn out to be a fire engine or a water truck."
>
> http://www.guardian.co.uk/Iraq/Story/0,2763,917323,00. html

My guess is that Iraq really doesn't have any WMD left. If some of it crops up, I would be suspicious that it's a plant. Blix commented yesterday that he "would be very interested" in knowing if the U.S. finds anything.

> In his appearance Sunday, on NBC's "Meet the Press," the vice president argued that "we believe [Hussein] has, in fact,

reconstituted nuclear weapons." But Cheney contradicted that assertion moments later, saying it was "only a matter of time before he acquires nuclear weapons." Both assertions were contradicted earlier by Mohamed El Baradei, director general of the International Atomic Energy Agency, who reported that "there is no indication of resumed nuclear activities."

http://www.msnbc.com/news/886806.asp

What is this, propaganda on the fly?

News is coming out right now [11:08 am PST] that fighting has begun in Basra. The war has begun.

What in the name of God has happened to us?

# March 20, 2003

Bombing in the Iraq started last night. A Cruise missile apparently attacked a "leadership target." Reports came that Saddam himself was targeted. The Red Cross reported this morning that one of the casualties was a Jordanian woman. The disposition of Saddam is still unknown.

Both China and Russia demanded an immediate halt to military action. Of course, a few other countries communicated support, such as Australia and Japan.

> Thursday began with American messages broadcast on Iraqi airwaves: "This is the day you have been waiting for."
>
> http://www.guardian.co.uk/worldlatest/story/0,1280,-2495846,00.html

I wonder how the people on the ground feel as they hear this message along side the bombs that are killing and wounding innocents.

All day I've read nothing but war talk. A few towns in Iraq have been taken. Maybe three or four oil wells have been set on fire. Bombs and missiles are dropping on Baghdad and various other locations. I hear that "shock and awe" are yet to come.

A few Iraqi troops have already surrendered. As expected, however, the Iraqi resistance is completely minimal--certainly less than the first Gulf war. So far, we received no attack from chemical agents, but the U.S. troops throw on the gas masks at the drop of a hat. Hence, the U.S. seems to overestimate Iraqi weaponry.

> Certainly we are better safe than sorry, but the consequence is more work and stress on the troops. A soldier can only

wear a chemical suit for a few hours before the heat becomes overwhelming. Perhaps heat overload could be an effective strategy for Iraq: keep scaring her foes with an air burst every hour or so for an indefinite period. This strategy will keep troops suited up. However, the Iraqis don't have the power to sustain even the most minimal resistance.

Saddam probably lost his power after the first Gulf war. He had a few well paid and trusted friends to keep him seated. Military loyalty is fragile to say the least. Probably certain forces are just waiting for the right moment to break free.

I agree with Senator Robert Byrd:

> Instead of reasoning with those with whom we disagree, we demand obedience or threaten recrimination. Instead of isolating Saddam Hussein, we seem to have isolated ourselves. We proclaim a new doctrine of preemption which is understood by few and feared by many. We say that the United States has the right to turn its firepower on any corner of the globe which might be suspect in the war on terrorism. We assert that right without the sanction of any international body. As a result, the world has become a much more dangerous place.
>
> http://www.antiwar.com/orig/byrd3.html
>
> Sorry, Robert, but no one is listening.
>
> "While this America settles in the mould of its vulgarity, heavily thickening to empire
>
> And protest, only a bubble in the molten mass, pops
>
> And sighs out, and the
>
> Mass hardens…"
>
> Robinson Jeffers

# March 21, 2003

The president returned to the White House and had dinner with First Lady Laura Bush and then relaxed in the living room. Around 8 p.m. Chief of Staff Andrew H. Card Jr. called to tell the President that Iraqi President Saddam Hussein was not complying with the President's ultimatum. The President went to the Oval Office just after 9:30 pm.

> Just before he went on the air, as aides were applying makeup, Bush was seen pumping his fist and telling an aide, "Feel good."
>
> http://www.latimes.com/la-war-countdown20mar2000342 9,0,153784.story

I can't profess to know what Bush meant by pronouncing the "feel good" comment.

In his speech Blair said:

> "We are asked now seriously to accept that in the last few years, contrary to all history and intelligence, [Saddam] decided unilaterally to destroy these weapons. I say such a claim is palpably absurd."

> It is, however, as we have described many times in our Media Alerts, the claim of UNSCOM weapons inspectors, who say that Iraq was "fundamentally disarmed" (90-95%) of its weapons of mass destruction (WMD) between 1991-98 without the threatening 'stick' of war - cooperation was in response to the 'carrot' of lifted sanctions. Amazingly, on the very brink of war, the resignation speech by Robin Cook,

leader of the House of Commons, contained the first ever mention we have seen in the media of this forbidden truth:

> "Iraq probably has no weapons of mass destruction in the commonly understood sense of the term."
>
> http://www.zmag.org/content/showarticle.cfm?SectionID-21&ItemID=3301

But, so what. We are at war to purportedly remove Iraq's WMD. Whether we find such weapons or not is immaterial at this point. We shall find whatever we need to find.

The "shock and awe" bombing has apparently begun.

> An entire division of the Iraqi army, numbering 8,000 soldiers, surrendered to coalition forces in southern Iraq Friday, Pentagon officials said.
>
> "I kind of felt sorry for them," said one U.S. military official speaking on condition of anonymity. "A lot of them looked hungry. They haven't been fed in a while."
>
> http://www.guardian.co.uk/worldlatest/story/0,1280,-299677,00.html
>
> Public approval of President Bush has surged after the start of the war with Iraq, but not to the levels of support his father enjoyed during the Persian Gulf War a dozen years ago, polls suggest.
>
> http://www.guardian.co.uk/worldlatest/story/0,1280,-2499673,00.html

Here we are at just the second day into this war and Iraqi soldiers have already lost their desire to fight. This is the scary enemy that Bush tried to convince us all that we should quake in fear over. Yeah, Iraq definitely shows the ability to conquer the world.

We are bombing the daylights out of Baghdad. The residents must be horrifically terrified.

# *March 23, 2003*

The world seems to be exploding in anger over our invasion of Iraq. Protests have particularly erupted in the Arabic countries. The level of anger boils and transforms into rage. I am pleased to say that my Pastor spoke with an urgent tone against this invasion. He said:

> I would also encourage us as individuals and as a nation to look, not just across the world to the minute by minute details of war, but to look deeply into our own souls and acknowledge there the mixed impurity of our motivations, the complicit contribution of our own agendas and policies, and the biased focus of who we choose to call enemy.

The Pastor asked us to pray. We are now seeing war's tragedy. Women and children are being injured and killed. Americans are being captured and killed.

> As he held a picture of this son, Waters-Bey's father, Michael said: "I want President Bush to get a good look at this, really good look here. This is the only son I had, only son." He then walked away in tears...

> http://www.thewalchannel.com/news/2056537/detail.html

This father expresses the anger and distress we have.

> As many as three U.S. missiles aimed at targets in Iraq may have landed in Iran, two officials at the Pentagon said Saturday.

http://www.foxnews.com/story/0,2933,81845,00.html

The accidents and collaterals are indeed with us.

I heard a report yesterday that a command tent of the 101st Airborne was attacked. One person died and seventeen were wounded. Apparently the suspect is an American soldier also with the 101st.

> "Let's go." Those were the words uttered by President Bush to Defense Secretary Donald Rumsfeld, at 7:12 p.m. EST Wednesday, that authorized the United States to begin war with Iraq...

http://www.cnn.com/2003/ALLPOLITICS/03/21/sprj.irq. tick.tock/index.html

And, not a single sole said no.

> Mr. Perle, who as chairman of the Defense Policy board has been a leading advocate of the United States' invasion of Iraq, spoke on Wednesday in a conference call sponsored by Goldman Sachs, in which he advised participants on possible investment opportunities arising from the war. The conference's title was "Implications of an Imminent War: Iraq Now. North Korea Next?"

http://nytimes.com/2003/03/21/business/21GLOB. html?pagewanted=2

I wonder if we'd be at war at all if Perle weren't advising the President. He looks for profit on the backs of the "poor slobs" who serve in the military. I have nothing but contempt for this person, and I reach into the depths of my soul to find a way to forgive him.

### Coalition of the Willing
### White House Source
### Countries Supporting the war in Iraq

| | |
|---|---|
| Afghanistan | Micronesia |
| Albania | Mongolia |
| Australia | Netherlands |
| Bulgaria | Nicaragua |
| Colombia | Palau |
| Costa Rica | Panama |
| Czech Republic | Philippines |
| Denmark | Poland |
| Dominican Republic | Portugal |
| El Salvador | Romania |
| Eritrea | Rwanda |

Estonia
Ethiopia
Georgia
Honduras
Hungary
Iceland
Italy
Japan
Kuwait
Latvia
Lithuania
Macedonia
No Comment.

Singapore
Slovakia
Soloman Islands
South Korea
Spain
Turkey
Uganda
United Kingdom
Uzbekistan

# March 24, 2003

A possible chemical weapons plant has been purportedly found near Najaf, Iraq. This plant resides in a southern Shi'ite area, and the plant exists in a southern no-fly zone. So, a military plant of this nature would seem very unlikely.

Was this plant the Al-Kufa Cement Factory, which was inspected on January 8, 2003? Other places in the Najaf area were also inspected, such as the Al-Qaqa state company. Mineral samples were taken at the time. I can't imagine that a factory as large as the one found could have been missed during the inspection of this area.

> Meanwhile, outside Basra, cases of rockets, giant anti-shipping mines and other ammunition piled in dozens of bunkers were found at the Az-Zubayr Heliport.

> Some of the boxes were clearly marked with the names of British manufacturers. One pile of boxes in a store housing rocket-propelled grenades bears the name of Wallop Industries Limited, based in Middle Wallop, Hampshire.

> http://news.independent.co.uk/world/middle_east/story.jsp?story=390162

> The UN Secretary-General Kofi Annan today warned of a humanitarian crisis in the Iraqi city of Basra, where coalition forces were involved in fierce fighting.

> Asked whether coalition forces were looking after the needs of the Iraqi people, Annan said he had been told by the Red

Cross that "the people in Basra may be facing a humanitarian disaster."

http://news.independent.co.uk/world/politics/story. jsp?story=390458

Kabul, Afghanistan-AP -- There's been a rare display of public anger in Afghanistan over the war in Iraq.

About one-thousand people protested in eastern Afghanistan today One military official says it was peaceful.

The U-S-backed Afghan government has said the use of force to disarm Iraq is justified but many Afghans oppose the war.

http://www.kait8.com/Global/story.asp?S=1194376

In this war no matter what direction we turn an enemy jumps out. In many cases that enemy is our own stupidity.

Some vehicles were still smoldering, and charred ribs were the only recognizable part of three melted bodies in a destroyed car lying in the roadside dust.

"It wasn't even a fair fight. I don't know why they don't just surrender," said Colonel Mark Hildenbrand, commander of the 937th Engineer Group. "When you're playing soccer at home, 3-2 is a fair score, but here it's more like 119-0."

http://www.reuters.com

With a hail of small arms fire and rocket-propelled grenades, Iraqi forces downed two Apache helicopters today and forced 30 other helicopters in their brigade back to their base.

The Apaches use a powerful radar, called the Longbow, that directs their Hellfire missiles. But the helicopters are suddenly coming under attack from relatively low-technology weaponry.

Saddam Hussein "is fighting an asymmetrical warfare," said Brig. Gen. Benjamin Freaklyi, assistant commander of the 101st Division. "This is not tank-on-tank fighting."

http://www.nytimes.com/2003/03/24

Technology doesn't always do the job.

# March 25, 2003

The war in Iraq now moves into its sixth day with U.S. troops bogged down in a sandstorm fifty miles south of Baghdad. I think Rumsfeld et al severely underestimated the resistance and will of the Iraqis. Some armchair generals are saying we invaded Iraq with too light a force.

> "The Secretary of Defense cut off the flow of Army units, saying this thing would be over in two days," said a retired senior general who has followed the evolution of the war plan. "He shut down movement of the 1st Cavalry Division and the1st Armored Division. Now we don't even have a nominal ground force."
>
> http://www.bayarea.com/mld/mercurynews/news/special_packages/iraq/5472430.htm

Even though the Iraqis have threatened use of chemicals if we attack Baghdad, we have yet to encounter chemical agents, nor have we found stores of them.

In the meantime, Halliburton won a contract to fight oil fires.

> The first contracts for rebuilding post-war Iraq have been awarded, and Vice President Dick Cheney's old employer, Halliburton Co., is one of the early winners.
>
> http://money.cnn.com/2003/03/25/news/companies/war_contracts/index.htm

> An Australian FA/18 Hornet pilot has refused an American command to bomb a target in Iraq in the first conflict

between the different rules governing the way the two allies make war.

http://www.nzherald.co.nz

The pilot refused not out of moral indignation, but because of a tougher set of rules that Australian pilot must follow in the conduct of war. The Australians are signatories of the Geneva Conventions of 1977, while the U.S. is not. These accords require absolute certainty that the target is indeed a proper military objective.

> Department of Defense officials said on Monday that no evidence of chemical weapons production had been found at a facility close to the southern Iraqi town of Najaf occupied by U.S. forces on Sunday.

http://news.ft.com

At least the DoD provided a negative report rather than a lie.

> Iran, which has reported several violations of its airspace by U.S. and British jets attacking Iraq, said on Monday it might fire on aircraft which enter its skies.

http://famulus.msnbc.com/FamulusIntl

> A U.S. special envoy rushed back to Turkey but failed to reach agreement Monday on Turkey's plans to send troops in north Iraq.

http://story.news.yahoo.com/news

> Syria protested to the U.S. and Britain last night after a U.S. missile killed five Syrian workers and injured 10 who were fleeing the war in a bus.

http://news.independent.co.uk/world/middle_east/story. jsp?story=390540

As we fight on, the war leaks into the neighboring countries.

> "We cannot know the duration of this war, yet we know its outcome: We will prevail," Bush, commander in chief of 300,000 troops in the Persian Gulf, told U.S. military personnel at the Pentagon.

> "The Iraq regime will be disarmed. The Iraq regime will be ended. The Iraq people will be free and our world will be more secure and peaceful," he said.

http://www.salon.com/news/wire/2003/03/25/war_
duration/index.html

What does prevail mean? What if this war takes a year or more to prevail? So far, the only disarmament that's occurred is conventional weapons. But, conventional weapons were not the basis for this war in Iraq, now was it? What sort of spin will Bush conjure up if we don't find WMD. Frankly, I don't want us to find any WMD. I want Bush to go down in history as the unfortunate buffoon that he is.

# March 26, 2003

I believe the Iraqis have decided to take some offensive measures.

A large contingent of Iraq's elite Republican Guard headed south in a 1000-vehicle convoy Wednesday toward U.S. Marines in central Iraq – an area that already has seen the heaviest fighting of the war. In Baghdad, Iraqi officials said two cruise missiles hit a residential area, killing 14 people.

http://www.guardian.co.uk/worldlatest/story/0,1280,-2511655,00.html

The Iraqi forces are using the sandstorm as a cover.

"They say that the Iraqi people are oppressed by the tyrant, must be liberated and given democracy. And look how they are trying to achieve this goal: by using the most powerful weapons in history," Ivanov said.

"What democracy are they talking about when they are trying to completely destroy the country? I strongly doubt that democracy can be enforced by the Tomahawk (cruise missiles)."

http://cnews.canoe.ca/CNEWS/World/2003/03/26/51392-ap.html

Igor Ivanov is the Russian Foreign Minister. The U.S. is accusing Russia of supplying Iraq with advanced weapons and electronic equipment.

Powell was responding to a question about an article in The New York Times on Sunday suggesting he resign on the grounds that President Bush had repudiated Powell's "deep suspicion of arrogant idealism."

http://www.reuters.com

Perhaps Powell will be the next major casualty of the Bush Administration. Powell goes on to deny that any disagreement exists between him and Bush.

As he did in the early days of military action in Afghanistan, Mr. Bush on Sunday assumed his role as "consoler in chief."

"I pray for God's comfort and God's healing powers, to anybody, coalition force, American, Brit, anybody who loses a life in this, in our efforts to make the world more peaceful and more free," he said.

http://www.washtimes.com/national/20030325-84895. htm

I wish Bush would spare us the syrupy gush. This war in Iraq mocks the idea of peace.

Today at about 8:40am, I heard Dr. Marshall Rosenberg being interviewed on KPFA (94.1 MHZ). He spoke about non-violent communications as applied to Bush and associates. He said that in order to communicate with Bush, the important process is not to demonize and create an image of Bush as an enemy. Rather, he suggests trying to understand what Bush needs to produce a sense of safety and security for himself along with people the world over. Once we understand the needs, then we can look at options to deliver them. Certainly non-violent options exist as we have already noted with regards to Iraq.

This was no member of the Baath Party speaking. This was a man with degrees from universities in Manchester and Birmingham. A colleague had an even more cogent point to make. "Our soldiers know they will not get a fair deal from the Americans," he said.

"It's important that they know this. We may not like our regime. But we fight for our country. The Russians did not like Stalin but they fought under him against the German invaders. We have a long history of fighting the colonial powers, especially you British. You claim you are coming to 'liberate' us. But you don't understand. What is happening now is we are starting a war of liberation against the Americans and the British."

http://argument.independent.co.uk/commentators/story.jsp?story=390867

The U.S. military has been forced to admit the 8,000 Iraqi soldiers they claimed to have captured last week are now battling British forces.

Iraq's 51st Infantry Division, which has about 200 tanks, is now engaged in the southern city of Basra.

http://www.ananova.com/news/story/sm_764618.html

FUBAR. That's how I classify this war so far. I feel sorry for the troops right now. They're being pushed through a living hell, and I see no end of it. We look so far like the biggest bungling idiots that ever slept in Washington.

We've had forty-seven coalition deaths so far, and hundreds of Iraqis have died.

I sent the following letter to the Mercury News:

Just a couple days after the war began we heard that 8000

Iraqi soldiers surrendered from Iraq's 51st Infantry Division.

This event didn't happen. British soldiers are now fighting this Iraqi unit near Basra. Of course, again the U.S. claimsthey received some faulty reports. First, let's not forget thatwar is FUBAR [I won't translate]. Second, U.S. and British troops are engaged in battle with not only Iraqi forces in the form of guerillas and plainclothes militia, but also withering sandstorms.

Our military command seriously underestimated and misjudged the battle conditions. Hence, our troops have been dangerously exposed now for seven days. Yes, that means no showers or soft beds. They're eating and breathing sand and bullets. And, the most difficult part of the fight is fifty miles ahead. Eventually, U.S. forces will prevail over Saddam's Iraq. But, I don't think any of us expected the price we will pay for the questionable result. After all, we haven't found a single weapon of mass destruction yet and forty-seven British and U.S. soldiers have died so far. Good morning, Saddam! That sounds a lot like, "Good morning, Vietnam!"

# March 27, 2003

GEORGE Bush ordered his 4th Infantry Division to the Gulf yesterday, a decision seen by critics as an admission that the original invasion force was too small and deployed too early.

> http://news.scotsman.com/topics.
> cfm?id=364032003&tid=518

In other words George and company were over confident and they screwed up. Now we're moving into a deeper, more expensive quagmire.

> Although reporters on the ground continue to deny, British Defence Secretary Geoff Hoon claimed Wednesday, March 26, that Iraqi militia have attacked their own citizens in the southern city of Basra after people staged an uprising against the regime.
>
> http://islamonline.net/english/News/2003/2003-03-26/article07.shtml

The truth continues to be a mystery.

> The young man wearing the brown shawl summed it up succinctly: "We want you to go back home. We do not want your American and British aid," he said, his eyes flashing with anger.
>
> If the British humanitarian taskforce had any doubts as to the legitimacy of his claims, the sudden burst of gunfire from a nearby building left no one in any doubt.

http://www.guardian.co.uk/Iraq/Story/0,2763, 922723,00.
html

Ugly Americanism. We thought we'd be welcomed with hugs and flowers. What seems to have happened looks like rejection.

> Solomon Islands Prime Minister Sir Allan Kemakeza yesterday said "thanks but no thanks" after hearing his nation had been shanghaied into the U.S.-led Coalition of the Willing.
>
> "The Government is completely unaware of such statements being made, therefore wishes to disassociate itself from the report," said Sir Allan.
>
> http://www.nzherald.co.nz/storydisplay.cfm?storyID=3300
> 727&thesection=news&thesubsec...

More exaggerations about who supports who.

I cancelled my cable TV service today. I wasn't getting a level of service that met my standards or interests. The service also includes Internet access. The cable network performed well, but support also did not meet my standards. Since, I'm in the business of delivering Internet services, and I must respond to trouble within a four-hour period. I expect that level of service from the private sector. Twenty-four or forty-eight hour response times do not even come close to my level of tolerance, especially when the programming is by in large propaganda.

In a sense I cut myself off from the war news by canceling this service. But, perhaps I also cut myself from supporting the war, and probably also from the protest movement. At least the electronic war that enters the living room will be off. I feel able to live without the email and web at home. However, I'm not sure my wife will handle this well, since she conducts classes using email. So, I'm sure I might be engaged in discussions soon that will entail reinstalling cable Internet services.

> "Everything will be measured by results," Rove said. "The victor is always right. History ascribes to the victor qualities that may or may not actually have been there. And similarly to the defeated."
>
> http://www.washingtonpost.com/ac2/wp-dyn/A14101-200
> 2Feb2?language=printer

The comment above was made by Karl Rove, advisor to the President. The Iraqis are ascribing the U.S. as the aggressor and brutal colonizer. And, some people are now looking at the Iraqis as victims of a cruel atrocity. I tend to ascribe to the victim's viewpoint because perhaps I feel victimized and I can identify with those who suffer under the conqueror's hands. Our Administration has this arrogant idea that we are the righteous ones regarding our invasion of Iraq. The majority of American people seem to be in agreement on this American-centric perspective. I don't agree with the Administration and I am trying to use Marshall Rosenberg's advice and not make an enemy out of Bush, et al. I should try to understand what the majority's needs and feelings are. However, I find making enemies a lot easier.

# March 28, 2003

Saddam Hussein donated hundreds of thousands of dollars to a Detroit church and received a key to the city more two decades ago, soon after he became president of Iraq.

Saddam's bond with Detroit started in 1979, when the Rev. Jacob Yasso of Chaldean Sacred Heart congratulated Saddam on his presidency. In return, Yasso said, his church received $250,000.

"He's very kind to Christians," Yasso said.

http://apnews.excite.com/article/20030326/D7Q11H0G0.html

Even though we demonize our enemies, no one is as bad as some would want us to think. I could demonize Bush at this point. He has invaded a foreign country unilaterally and civilians have been killed. He has decided to remove the U.S. from the Kyoto and ABM agreements. He was witness to power company fraud in California and he had a significant business relationship with Ken Lay. His economic program has driven the country into historic levels of deficit spending. In just two years in office he has already led the U.S. into two major wars both of which seem to have no conclusion in sight. Unemployment has reached a 12-year high. Americans have fewer freedoms due to the Patriot and Homeland Security Acts. The majority of Americans didn't vote for Bush. He achieved the Presidency through a Supreme Court ruling that was clearly divided by party lines. I could go on and on about Bush, until the list leads to the supposition that this President is incompetent at the very best, or criminal at the worst.

> President Bush pledged again yesterday to rid Iraq of "weapons of terror," but coalition forces have so far failed to find proof of Iraqi biological or chemical weapons a week after the start of the U.S.-led invasion.
>
> http://www.washingtonpost.com/ac2/wp-dyn/A34232-2003March26

What if we don't find WMD in Iraq? What sort of demon do Bush and crowd become? Would the American people find the wisdom to elect this man out of office? Of course, I would like him out anyway, but apparently I'm in the minority right now.

> Ulan Bator, Mongolia – A senior diplomat [Ann Wright] at the U.S. Embassy in Mongolia has resigned in protest over Washington's decision to wage war in Iraq. . .
>
> http://story.news.yahoo.com/news

This is the third diplomat who has resigned due to Bush's foreign policy. This is the breakdown of loyalty according to some people in the government, but loyalty and morality often conflict. A few people will muster the courage and risk everything to express their beliefs. But, three people mean nothing in the vast scheme of things. Mass rebellion only occurs when the grievances become so overwhelming that the public sees no recourse but to separate from the government. The government can do almost anything if the public's livelihood remains intact.

> NASSIRIYAH, Iraq – U.S. Marines, moving through this still-congested city, opened fire at anything that moved Tuesday, leaving dozens of dead in their wake, at lease some of them civilians.
>
> http://www.miami.com/mld/miamiharold/news/world/5483028.htm

If we can't distinguish the enemy from the general population, and the invading troops feel threatened, then the first option that comes to mind is to shoot. Should we prosecute the troops who shoot indiscriminately, or should we impeach the commander in chief? Or, should we do neither? Perhaps we should hope that no one will really notice a little atrocity here and there, if the total effort achieves a great and noble cause. Unfortunately the official basis for the war still remains unproven; that is the discovery of WMD. Perhaps by the time we discover the WMD—if it exists—we shall have forgotten the battle traumas and errors.

> "The enemy we're fighting against is different from the one
> we'd war-gamed against," said General William S. Wallace,
> Commander of V Corps. [http://story.news.yahoo.com]

Are we supposed to be sympathetic with Bush and the generals for not thinking of the guerrilla war possibility? Our intelligence and war preparations were way off the mark in this war. We underestimated and we misunderstood our enemy. So, what are we doing but the exact same thing we did in Vietnam: bring in more troops, bomb harder, dial up the rain of death. From the outside observer this war is an incredible bungle. If pitted against an overwhelming force involving air power and bombardment, the only possible strategy for the enemy is to disburse forces outside of the bombing area and harass the invaders with hit and run tactics. Why was this not an obvious possibility, especially among generals who served in Vietnam? According to Lt. General Wallace, the Army trained against many other possible fighting tactics except the most obvious. This serious error in judgment is an outcome of arrogance, and, the ignorance of our Administration. Clearly, Rumsfeld et al seemed to believe that bomb tonnage would shock the Iraqis into quick capitulation. However, the bombs didn't work in Vietnam. Why should they work in Iraq?

I am so upset about this war that I spend time looking for only those pieces of news that point out the mistakes and inconsistencies of our Administration. I seem to find plenty of examples.

> The 'Sir Galahad', a British naval supply ship, docked at
> around 3:30pm with 232 tons of water and 150 tons of rice,
> lentils, cooking oil, tomato paste, chick peas, sugar, powdered
> milk and tea, and medicine. For the people of southern Iraq
> who have been without fresh water or electricity since the
> American-led war began 10 days ago its arrival came not a
> moment too soon.
>
> http://news.independent.co.uk/world/middle_east/story.
> jsp?story=391821

Interesting that this ship bears the name of Galahad, the knight who searched for the Holy Grail. He is described by Tennyson (*Sir Galahad*) as the classic knight in gleaming armor with the strength of ten men and with a heart of purity that when his battle ends . . . "Perfume and flowers fall in showers,/ That lightly ran from ladies' hands."

The grail, of course, is the sacred cup that held the blood of Jesus as he hung from the cross. This cup held the power of everlasting and bounteous life. Perhaps some in our Administration believed America to be figuratively Sir Galahad. We would smite the enemy, feed the hungry, and then be lauded with flowers. Unfortunately when Sir Galahad arrived in Iraq, her armor appeared very tarnished indeed.

# March 29, 2003

The war rolls on into its tenth day. The *San Jose Mercury* writes today that aides to Bush didn't convincingly present the realities of Iraqi resistance. Apparently the CIA knew what lay ahead for the invasion, but Bush chose to listen to Cheney and Rumsfeld who believed Saddam's forces would collapse after the "shock and awe" bombing campaign.

The Iraqi strategy, however, seems to follow classic guerilla tactics as defined by Russian Maskerovka, Maoism, and the ideas of Ho Chi Minh. This military approach consists of blending with the local populace, planting false information, masquerading, and hiding. The guerrillas attack from the flanks when troops are most vulnerable. They engage in terrorism to cast aspersions and blame on the invaders. They will use decoys to draw and waste the opponent's ammunition. They never remain in one place for long and will disperse widely so as not to be easily located or vulnerable to bombs.

Classical field tactics work poorly in a guerrilla environment because the enemy isn't concentrated or exposed to a large battlefield force. If the opponents are concerned about collateral damage, then guerrillas can easily stay alive by taking shelter in homes and public places.

Fighting a guerrilla war is very difficult. Saddam certainly has experience in this type of battle and he has made use of one of the most brutal, but effective, counter-guerrilla techniques. He didn't discriminate between a guerrilla and the locals. He killed and tortured anybody who had even the slightest suspicion. Disagreement and dissent brought death. This type of atrocious strategy serves two purposes: it eliminates opposition and terrorizes those left behind in order to prevent insurrections. Less brutal tactics are certainly available, but require more time, well organized infiltration forces, intelligence, and lightening fast attacks on unsuspecting insurgents.

Of course, I'm not in Iraq. I criticize from a comfortable distance. Not only is my behavior macho but stupid. I feel completely sorry for the soldiers serving in Iraq.

What a barbaric condition for the youth of our world. I wish to God that I could have stopped this fight.

# March 30, 2003

I saw James Baker on the news this morning. He kept reiterating that our invasion of Iraq is absolutely the right thing to do. Of course, I'll never agree that invading Iraq is "right." What is right in the case of Iraq? Bush established rightness primarily on the basis of WMD proliferation to terrorists. Hence, WMD need to be found and so far nothing has been found. The other premise is the removal of the evil and dangerous dictator. Will Bush have the patience to settle the many post-Saddam conflicts without using force? His record for peaceful conflict resolution is not too good.

# March 31, 2003

I wake up in the morning to war. My anxiety level rises as we see more casualties. Over 100 U.S. soldiers are dead or missing. The numbers go up every day we sit 50 fifty miles from Baghdad. My thoughts come in blacks and whites. The war is either right or wrong. We should engage the Iraqis or pull our troops out. Bush is doing a good job or he's not. The protest movement is useful or useless.

I find myself with a lot of free floating anger; the root of which seems to be my feeling of powerlessness. We have lost our voice now that we are crawling in war's quagmire: wars that have no end.

> Bagram Air Base, Afghanistan – The deaths of two U.S. soldiers in southern Afghanistan point to a rebel resurgence following the start of the war in Iraq that may lead to a wider U.S. campaign against pro-Taliban and al-Qaida fighters.
>
> http://www.bayarea.com/mld/mercurynews/news/world/5523162.htm

We were supposed to end Bin Laden's rule and stamp out the al-Qaeda. Such things don't seem to work out, and those who try to debate and draw our policies to question are alienated.

> "Those of us who raise our hands in question here or speak out in dissent seem to get immediately attacked as being unpatriotic," said Farr, 61, a 10-year veteran of the House of Representatives. "We know what we believe and we say outright we support the troops. . . but it's spin doctors who

are also out there criticizing us, saying you can't be both, you can't be a patriot and not be 100 percent supportive of the United States."

http://www.bayarea.com/mld/mercurynews/news/
world/5523137.htm

When I watched the news this morning, I only heard how wonderfully the invasion is proceeding. Saddam Hussein, of course, is nowhere to be seen. Threats of chemical attack abound, but no evidence of chemical weapons has been found.

The time is 10:19am (PST). I note that the DOW is down -147.90 to 7997.80. The DOW hasn't been this low for a long time.

Charlie—one of my work colleagues--just came into my office and noted that a recent bomb that hit Baghdad was intended to destroy a large bunker filled with chemical weapons. Apparently Saddam and one of his sons were in the bunker. Both supposedly died. Charlie says his friend works in high places within the Defense Department. Of course, my position is not to believe a thing, especially rumors that get passed around the coffeemaker.

> Washington – We're shocked that the enemy forces don't observe the rules of war. ...Why is all this a surprise again? I know our hawks avoided serving in Vietnam, but didn't they, like, read about it?
>
> http://www.nytimes.com/2003/03/30/opinion/30DOWD.
> html (opinion by Maureen Dowd)

The generals probably aren't shocked, but I believe they were overruled by an overzealous group of white males: Rumsfeld, Wolfowitz, Perle, Cheney, and Bush.

> "We know where they are, they [WMD] are in the area around Tikrit and Baghdad and east, west, south, and north of that," he [Rumsfeld] said.
>
> http://www.guardian.co.uk/Iraq/Story/0,2763,926187,00.
> html

Listen, Rumsfeld, you arrogant son-of-a-bitch, if you don't know, say so. Yet, we have even more evidence of arrogance.

> Of the 30 members of the Defense Policy Board, the government-appointed group that advises the Pentagon, at

least nine have ties to companies that have won more than $76 billion in defense contracts in 2001 and 2002.

The companies. . .include Boeing, TRW, Northrop Grumman, Lockheed Martin, and Booz Allen Hamilton. . .

http://www.publicintegrity.org

Of course, Richard Perle was the chair of this board until recently when the conflict of interest questions start to weigh too heavily. Seems to me that this board could profit greatly from a war. And, this board would do everything in its power to argue for a large international conflict, as Richard Perle did.

# *April 1, 2003*

In the area near Hilla, Iraq 48 civilians were killed. Seven civilians were killed near Karabala. In Tanabiyak 11 children, 7 women, and 2 men were killed. Coalition troops killed all these people. The "collateral" casualties climb day by day. For every American that dies, five civilians meet the same tragedy.

No WMD appears to date and no Saddam Hussein. We continue to hear about death, destruction, deprivation, and lies. Perhaps when we determine that no WMD exists, we will be outraged enough to get rid of the maniacs in Washington.

Journalist Peter Arnett was fired from NBC for having an interview with Iraqi TV, during which he said that the American military strategy had failed. The fact that Arnett would be fired is predictable. But, the example exemplifies that national news media definitely puts restrictions on its employees' mouths.

I suppose that the Iraqi interview was not in the line of NBC duties. He probably did the interview in his own time and took the liberty of stating an opinion—an opinion, I might add, felt by many.

Geraldo Rivera was also tossed out of Iraq because he apparently gave away troop positions during a broadcast. Of course, Rivera seems to be part of the Fox News propaganda machine. Arnett tries to present his honest impressions, even though upsetting to the Administration.

I imagine within the next week or two the war will show some breakthrough. Baghdad will likely capitulate. The fight might stop. I don't believe the Iraqi people will have the will to fight.

> Sergeant Eric Schrumpt is a Marine sharpshooter in Iraq.
> According to the March 29 issue of the New York Times,

Schrumpf and his fellow sharpshooters sometimes hold their fire when a lot of civilians are in the vicinity. But when few civilians are around, they fire away.

Schrumpf recalled one incident where an Iraqi soldier was standing near a woman.

"I'm sorry, but the chick was in the way," he said.

http://www.progressive.org/webes03/wx033103.html

War somehow sanctions the amoral demon in people. I am continually reminded of Stanley Milgram's psychological experiments at Yale during the early 1960s. He staged a person in a fake electric chair. The subject of the experiment was asked to question the "victim." If he/she answered the question incorrectly, the subject would give the victim an electrical shock. The voltage was increased every time the victim answered incorrectly. Of course, the victim would never get the right answer and each shock would cause an increasing display of agony consisting of screams and appeals to stop the experiment. The white-coated authority in charge, however, continued to direct the subject to proceed in spite of the apparent escalating torture.

Very few subjects resisted the authority's direction. Most would proceed to the point in which the victim acted dead. Yet, what seems more disturbing about our personality is that we find a sort of pleasure in the torture upon others. The German word for this behavior is *schadenfreude*.

# April 2, 2003

My friend Dave sent me this message with a quote from *Catch 22*.

> The liberation business brings to mind a passage from Joseph Heller's Catch 22, the timeless war satire set in WWII. The Americans have recently captured Italy and a young American G.I. named Nately is visiting a whorehouse in liberated Palermo, Sicily, where he gets into a conversation with the ancient proprietor.

> The old man describes the proper way to greet liberators, of any stripe. "...I was a fascist when Mussolini was on top, and I'm an anti-fascist now that he has been deposed. I was fanatically pro-German when the Germans were here to protect us against the Americans, and now that the Americans are here to protect us against the Germans I am fanatically pro-American. I can assure you, my outraged young friend" –the old man's knowing, disdainful eyes shown even more effervescently as Nately stuttering dismay increased—"that you and your country will have no more loyal partisan in Italy than me – but only as long as you remain in Italy."

> "But," Nately cried out in disbelief, "you're a turncoat! A time-server! A shameful, unscrupulous opportunist!"

> "I am a hundred and seven years old," the old man reminded him suavely.

Now we are 25 miles from Baghdad. The glorious U.S. Army is putting the pinch on the city. We're inside the "Red Zone," the area threatened with chemical weapons.

The first Iraqi suicide bomber was Ali Jaffer Mousa Hamadi al-Nomani. He was a Shiite Muslim, which is ironic because we expected the Shiites to rise against Saddam once the Americans opened the path to Baghdad. Perhaps we now can see that the many diverse groups in Iraq have unexpected diversity within themselves.

I picked the following from http://nowar.greenpeace.org/images/scan1_ 1g.gif:

03/31/2003 16:40 FAX [Typed by Author]

SUBJECT:  Possible UNCA and CHR Sessions

Possible UNCA and CHR Sessions

Herewith the text of a FAX received from [Text deleted] in the US Embassy, regarding points discussed by the US Ambassador and [Text deleted] on 18 March 2003 for your information.

- Some members of the General Assembly have been discussing holding a General Assembly Emergency Session on Iraq should the Security Council not produce an additional Chapter VII resolution on the subject.

- We urge you to oppose such a session, and either to vote against or abstain if the matter is brought to a vote.

- We deeply regret that the Security Council was unable to agree on a new resolution to enforce UNSCR 1441. However, the Council remains seized of this matter. For this reason alone, the GA must refrain from taking up this matter.

- If necessary the US will meet its responsibilities and lead a coalition to ensure that Iraq is disarmed. We have the authority to do so, in view of the "all necessary means authorization contained in Resolution 678 and the material breach of Iraq's disarmament obligations under Resolutions 687 and 1441.

- Given the highly charged atmosphere, the United States would regard a General Assembly session on Iraq as unhelpful, and as directed against the United States. Please know that this questions as well as your position on it is important to the US.

- A General Assembly session could also further reinforce Iraq's belief that it has divided the international community and  is under no obligation to comply with Security Council resolutions.

- Finally, we are concerned that the staging of such a divisive session could be of additional harm to the UN.

Apparently the U.S. is trying to prevent a UN General Assembly meeting regarding the war in Iraq.

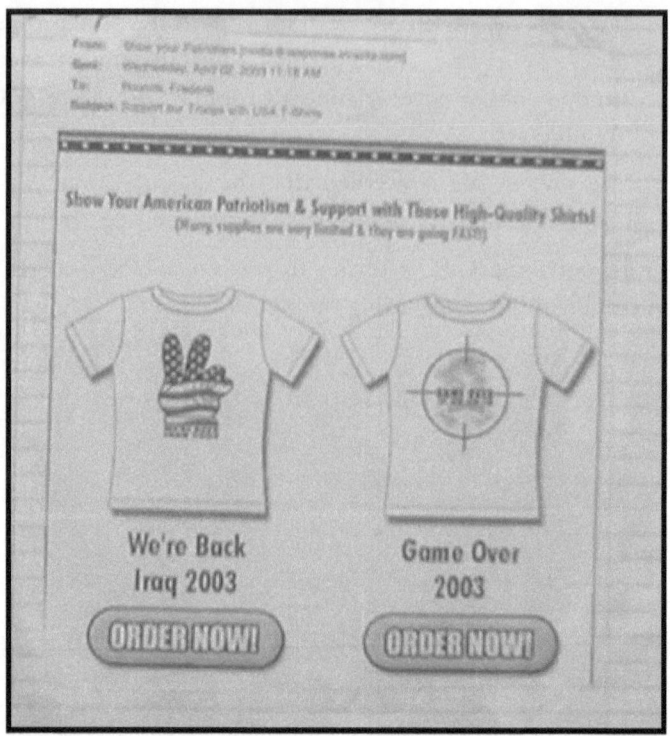

I received the above message today. This spam is the type of jingoistic capitalism that America is plagued with.

The Marines discovered on their way through Numaniyah, Iraq that the defenders had quickly abandoned their positions. They left behind their weapons and ammunition. Some Iraqi soldiers were seen tearing off their clothes and putting on civilian dress. Of course, the Marines are also drawing closer to Baghdad. On the surface the Iraqis appear to be retreating or deserting. But, another possibility could be a feint maneuver.

The idea is to draw invading troops into a vulnerable position then attack. The approach would be to reverse the concentration. Draw the invader into the city. Then swing to the rear of the U.S. forces. This maneuver would put U.S. troops at a significant disadvantage if supply lines were cut off. Yet, I doubt if the Iraqis would be able to pull this off because they would need to have more control of the transportation routes.

A more likely case is that the Iraqis have lost the will to fight. The indications are that the Iraqis not only don't have WMD, they lack sufficient conventional weapons and forces. Where's the Iraqi aircraft or even tanks?

# April 3, 2003

We have moved to the gates of Baghdad. Perhaps distances of six miles remain and we will reach the city's center. Apparently Saddam Airport has been captured already. U.S. troops have met very little resistance so far. Why? Soldiers' bodies lay around everywhere, each possessing a gas mask.

Is a gas attack still planned? Or, are the Iraqis afraid that we might retaliate with gas. The U.S. military often uses tear gas. I can't imagine the Iraqi military being capable of staging a gas attack at this point. The local military units don't have the visual capability to see where U.S. troops are concentrated in order to make best use of chemical weapons.

Unless some surprises lay in store as we enter the city [see Robert Fisk, www.independent.uk.co, 4/3/03], the war looks over. The Iraqi Army seems to have lost its fight. No one knows who's in charge. Now what?

I don't expect a great general to surrender. Apparently some of the generals have disappeared, such as Chemical Ali, the general who coordinated the gassing of the Kurds. Hence, a WMD attack seems even less likely. At some point we'll find out, so why guess.

> The experts also say using shells and rockets to target U.S. troops or to contaminate approaches to Baghdad would not be very effective.

> Chemical weapons "are of limited military utility and carry very high political and diplomatic cost," said Joseph Cirincione, a weapons-proliferation specialist with the Carnegie Endowment of International Peace. "They

wouldn't stop the advance. . . .But they could hurt Saddam's now-flourishing image as an Arab hero."

http://www.bayarea.com/mld/mercurynews/news/special_ packages/iraq/5547801.htm

So, maybe some types of WMD are not the terrible threat we all thought. Of course, we realize that chemical agents in an enclosed space, such as buildings or subways, are extremely dangerous. However, chemical weapons on the battlefield may not be as effective depending on the weather and concentration of troops.

# April 4, 2003

Reverend Franklin Graham, son of Evangelist Billy Graham, is waiting until the war dies down before his troupe of fundamentalist Christians invades Iraq. His Group, Samaritans Purse, will bring food and Bibles to the Muslims. Unfortunately Reverend Graham has accused Islam of being a "wicked, violent" religion. I look at Graham as just more contamination for the Iraqis to live with.

> This lack of progress among the weapons-hunters is reflected in the Bush administration's decision to play down its goal of ridding Iraq of its biological and chemical arms.
>
> On the second day of the war, Secretary of Defense Donald H. Rumsfeld listed the goal of finding, securing and destroying what the administration asserts are Iraq's weapons of mass destruction as second in importance only to the goal of toppling Saddam Hussein's government.
>
> But a week later, Victoria Clarke, the Pentagon spokeswoman, put the capture of "terrorist sheltered in Iraq" and the collection of "intelligence on terrorist networks" at the top of the list of the administration's war objectives.
>
> http://www.nytimes.com/2003/04/04/international/worldspecial/04CHEM.html

Why did I suspect this spin would begin to happen? We made a gigantic effort to convince the world that Saddam needed to be disarmed. But, I guess I can't expect the world to be as outraged as I am. I can't expect governments to live by a set of consistent values, constitutions, or laws.

# *April 5, 2003*

U.S. troops have now moved into Baghdad. To accomplish this campaign we have expended to date 65-million gallons of gasoline, lost 100 American lives, 600 Iraqi civilians, and God know how many Iraqi soldiers. We continue to search for WMD, and we have found nothing so far.

Inside my mind I ask myself why I'm so obsessively opposed to this war? Why do I want Bush to be punished and humiliated for invading Iraq? I look at my past: I dutifully served in the illegal and immoral Vietnam War. I have seen endless crime and excess in business and government. And, finally, I have watched so much of this corruption pass by without any outrage against and consequences for the perpetrators.

I have achieved such a level of cynicism that I firmly believe Bush will never experience accountability for an illegal war and crimes against humanity. Rather, he will be re-elected.

> "One thing that's really great about our country is there are thousands of people who pray for me that I'll never see and be able to thank."
>
> George W. Bush
> March 6, 2003

I hear Bush is a recovering drunk, but I think he's replaced alcohol with another form of intoxicant: power.

# April 6, 2003

Wolfowitz appeared on the news today. He claimed that he wanted America to be seen as liberators. I wonder how many Iraqi mothers feel that Americans are liberators as they see their children dying.

The headline of the *SJ Mercury* this morning is "U.S. Sets Stage for Showdown." Our minds seemed tuned into reality news, but we've covered the "reality" with images of the wild west. Perhaps images of an American fantasy on the streets of Tombstone makes the war understandable: a clear battle of good against evil as Bush would have us believe.

I keep coming back, however, to the fundamental justification for this war: WMD. Interestingly, South Africa noted today [*SJ Mercury, Perspective*]:

> "...For the allies, if they topple Saddam, but fail to produce evidence of the weapons, their personal and political credibility will be fatally undermined."

> The Sowetan
> Johannesburg

Isreal's *Jerusalem Post* also asks the question of what to do if WMD are not found. Yet, this newspaper's answer is simply to redefine the primary objective as a quest for Iraqi "justice and freedom."

So, the argument will always be present. We know what got us into the war, but as the evidence seems to show, we eventually may need another reason to quell public confusion over our preemptive actions. We now see the propaganda to demonize Saddam's regime switching into high gear.

# April 7, 2003

Today both NPR and the *NY Times* reported today the discovery of potential chemical weapons at 9:00am. The find consisted of 20 missiles containing Sarin and Mustard gas warheads. The NY Times reported that oil drums were found in the Karabala area. Some of the drums apparently contained nerve and mustard gases. Initial testing, however, was inconclusive. So was Bush right, or was he lucky? We may know in a few days.

But, as usual confusion exists depending on what you read. The *SJ Mercury* reported the same story of chemical agents as the *NY Times*. The *Mercury* reported that a dozen soldiers from the 101st Airborne were evacuated because they were experiencing symptoms of exposure to nerve agents. The *NY Times* described these soldiers as having been exposed to tear gas, or CN.

In addition, another story in the *Mercury* reported that Marines were instructed that they could remove their chemical protective clothing. Of course, some of the chemicals were found in a agricultural warehouse. Hence, we may have discovered pesticides and weed killers.

Over lunch, I learned from the Guardian that the "dozen" men evacuated for chemical exposure had heat stroke. They were not exposed to a chemical agent. And, ABC news reported that the chemicals we found are pesticides.

> A facility near Baghdad that a U.S. officer had said might finally be "smoking gun" evidence of Iraqi chemical weapons production turned out to contain pesticide, not sarin gas as feared.

> http://www.abc.net.au/news/justin/nat/newsnat-8apr2003-13.htm

Robert Novak comments [www.townhall.com/columnists/robertnovak/rn20030407.shtml] that the primary justification for the Iraq invasion was to destroy an evil regime. The secondary mission is to disarm Saddam of WMD. I also saw a CNN ticker tape yesterday about 9:00am that Centcom had reported that locating WMD was not its primary mission.

So, the spin is starting with not only the political pundits, but also the military information channel. What spin will come from the White House now that Baghdad is nearly sacked and no WMD has been used or found to date?

> "On the American side, there is a temptation now to punish those who were against us on the conflict and to try to divide Europe so that we can work the European split in such a way that it's advantageous to American policy," said Robert Kagan of the Carnegie Endowment for International Peace.

> http://www.gaurdian.co.uk/worldlatest/story/0,128i0,-2540815,00.html

Robert Kagan is Donald Kagan's brother. These two individuals, plus father, Frederick, seem to be spokespeople for a rather insidious group, The Project for the New American Century:

> American foreign and defense policy is adrift. Conservatives have criticized the incoherent policies of the Clinton Administration. They have also resisted isolationist impulses from within their own ranks. But conservatives have not confidently advanced a strategic vision of America's role in the world. They have not set forth guiding principles of American foreign policy. They have allowed differences over tactics to obscure potential agreement on strategic objectives. And they have not fought for a defense budget that would maintain American security and advance American interests in the new century.

> http://www.newamericancentury.org/statementofprinciples.htm

The above quote cast a little aspersion on the existing conservatives in government. But, the offered solution seems to be even further to the right than the general conservative.

> Our aim is to remind Americans of these lessons and to draw their consequences for today. Here are four consequences:

- We need to increase defense significantly if we are to carry out our global responsibilities today and modernize our armed forces for the future;

- We need to strengthen our ties to democratic allies and to challenge regimes hostile to our interests and values;

- We need to promote the cause of political and economic freedom abroad;

- We need to accept responsibility for America's unique role in preserving and extending an international order friendly to our security, our prosperity, and our principles.

Such a Reaganite policy of military strength and moral clarity may not be fashionable today. But it is necessary if the United States is to build on the successes of this past century and to ensure our security and our greatness in the next.

And even more insidious:

The only acceptable strategy is one that eliminates the possibility that Iraq will be able to use or threaten to use weapons of mass destruction. In the near term, this means a willingness to "undertake military action."

[same reference as above quote]

The signatories of the above document are such people as Donald Rumsfeld, Jeb Bush, Dick Cheney, Dan Quayle, Paul Wolfowitz, Steve Forbes, Eliot Abrams, and William Bennett. The conclusion I draw from the New American Century is that growing military might is the answer to our foreign policy. I think the Soviet Union is a good example of a country that consumed itself in building one of the world's largest military arsenals. By so doing the Russian economy ultimately collapsed.

William Bennett was Secretary of Education under Reagan. He was the man who made the impressive scientific remark "[homosexuality] takes 30 years off your life." I'm concerned that this is individual has Bush's ear.

# *April 8, 2003*

American News:

> V Corps Headquarters, in northern Kuwait, April 7 – American soldiers searching an empty military camp in the Karabala area have found several drums that, according to preliminary tests, may contain deadly nerve agents and mustard gas.

> http://www.nytimes.com/2003/04/08/international/worldspecial/08CHEM.html

Foreign News:

> Captain Adam Mastrianni, a military intelligence officer for the U.S. 101st Airborne Division's aviation brigade, said that after comprehensive tests, all that had been discovered was pesticide.

> Capt. Mastrianni added: "They thought it was a nerve agent. That's what it tested. But it is pesticide."

> http://www.news.scotsman.com/ijnternational.cfm?id=410632003

Which report is the correct one? I would tend to believe the foreign news because the article quotes an actual human being who apparently followed the testing.

We also haven't heard much about the 20 missiles with chemical warheads. I would imaging these weapons could be checked for chemical agents. But, my suspicion is that here too no chemical agents were found.

I made the mistake of watching the TV news last night. Cameras were focused for hours on an A-10 jet fighter flying over Baghdad. Ad nauseam conversations about Saddam Hussein's disposition dragged on until I was thoroughly convinced that we may never know what happened to him because his suspected location was completely obliterated by four bunker buster bombs. Apparently Saddam was visiting a restaurant with his sons. The restaurant was bombed to the point in which the only way to determine who the victims were is to find microscopic pieces of bodies and perform DNA tests. Of course, other rumors abound that Saddam escaped Baghdad several days ago and then he headed for Tikrit.

Watching the news is a study in depression. I cannot fathom in my mind how we as a country could convince our youth to decimate a country against the tenants of international law and the will of most of the world [according to the UN]. We have yet to be threatened by WMD and we still haven't found any real evidence, and if we do find a cache here or there what difference would it make? The weapons weren't used and, so far, the WMD don't appear to be stored in any arsenal ready for immediate use. We overwhelmed a country, killed many civilians for a cause that's been difficult to justify. I would want the justification to be more clear and identifiable. At present, I am so angry at our government that I want some higher power to bring this bunch of "war criminals" [Bush et al] to justice. Perhaps we're all lucky that the only higher power is God and God forgives and isn't vengeful. I imagine, however, that if Iraq turns into another prolonged war like Vietnam, then the higher power will be time and our terrible and unjustifiable experience of loss.

# April 9, 2003

The war now seems to be drawing to a type of ending. We see the remnants of Saddam's power being destroyed, such as tanks pulling down statues, and Saddam's posters being ripped from walls.

> "Freedom's taste is unquenchable," said White House spokesman Ari Fleisher. "You're seeing what you see in mankind everywhere, given a chance to be free."

> http;//www.cnn.com/2003/WORLD/meast/0409/sprj.irq.war.main/index.html

I wonder if Fleischer is including the looting and other general lawlessness that's now filling the streets of Baghdad. I saw an image of four men fighting over a sledge hammer to determine who would get to bash Saddam's statue.

We also see the victors gloat.

> "We are hopeful that a number of regimes will draw the appropriate lesson from Iraq that the pursuit of weapons of mass destruction is not in the national interest," Bolton said.

> He called the pursuit of nuclear, chemical or biological weapons programs a terrorist threat and said it "will remain our priority to achieve a peaceful elimination of these programs so that supporters of terrorism cannot use them against innocent people."

> http://www.washingtonpost.com/wp-dyn/articles/A63436-2003Apr9.html

John Bolton is the Undersecretary of State for Arms Control and Internal Security. I wonder what Bolton means by his remarks. I note that the suspicious barrels found in an agricultural warehouse had French writing on them. Does this mean we'll be invading France soon? Apparently the old chemical rounds that were found by the UN inspectors had Italian and Russian markings on them. So, I imagine we should target these countries at some point; maybe after Yemen, which imports missiles from North Korea.

Of course the elephant in the room keeps appearing.

> Well into the war that was supposed to rid Iraq of its alleged stockpile of weapons of mass destruction, a senior British official admitted on Saturday that no chemical, biological or nuclear weapons of mass destruction may after all be found.

> Making a startling confession in a radio interview, British Home Secretary, David Blunkett, added in the same breath that he would in any case rejoice the "fall" of Saddam Hussein and his regime—regardless of whether any weapons of mass destruction were found in Iraq or not.

> http://english.aljazeera.net/topics/article.asp?cu_ no=1&item_no=1858&version=1&templatge_i...

The *SJ Mercury* had an editorial about making sure that not only does WMD need to be found to make this war legitimate, but any stores of WMD must be certified by an international body, such as the UN. I'm convinced that since these special weapons haven't been used, then the presence of WMD still doesn't make a significant argument for invading Iraq.

Also, I see reports from *Al Jazeera*. I'm uncertain of the credibility of this news source. It seems to be the source that reported with certainty that the recent discovery of chemical-filled drums is merely pesticide. The American and British sources claim more testing needs to occur.

I keep hearing that the real test for patriotism is whether you support the troops or not. "Support the troops" is one of those jingoistic phrases that when given a modicum of thought, fails to retain consistency.

Do I want our troops to be an instrument of an ambiguous, possibly illegal, and outwardly failed foreign policy? No. Do I want soldiers to sacrifice their moral standards in this war? No. Do I want soldiers to struggle perhaps many years later over the question of whether their actions were justified? No. Do I want the soldiers to come home to a critical and possibly hostile country? No. Unfortunately the foundation for the soldiers to experience doubts has already been laid in this war. We went into this war with unanswered questions. And, now that we have thoroughly savaged Iraq we still have not resolved those questions. When we get over the triumph, I wonder if we'll feel any shame for what we've done. Americans imposed the Nuremberg trials on the Nazis. Will we impose the same examination on ourselves?

# April 10, 2003

"In removing the terror regime from Iraq, we send a very clear message to all groups that operate by means of terror and violence against the innocent. The United States and or coalition partners are showing that we have the capacity and the will to wage war on terror and to win decisively."

VP Dick Cheney

http://www.upi.com/view.cfm?StoryID=20030409-043736-4887r

And, certainly the way we deal with terror and violence is to return with our brand of terror and violence against innocents who happen to be in the wrong place at the wrong time. In the case of Iraq the unresolved argument exists over whether we are threatened by Saddam's regime. As we invaded Iraq we have encountered no WMD, no tanks, and no aircraft. One of the rifles found in a weapons cache was made in 1895. How could we perceive a serious threat from Saddam's regime?

"More people are going to be killed; let there be no doubt. This is not over, despite all the celebrations on the street," Rumsfeld said.

[Same reference as above]

What a comfort to know that more people will be killed.

Baghdad, Iraq—U.S. Marines may have found weapons-grade plutonium in a massive underground facility discovered beneath Iraq's Al Tuwaitha nuclear complex, and embedded reporter told Fox News Thursday.

Capt. John Seegar, a combat engineer commander from Houston, is currently running the operation in Al Tuwaitha. "I've never seen anything like it, ever," he told the Tribune-Review. "How did the world miss all of this? Why couldn't they see what was happening here?"

http://www.foxnews.com/story/0,2933,83821,00.html

Vienna, Austria (AP) – American troops who suggested they uncovered evidence of an active nuclear weapons program in Iraq unwittingly may have stumbled across known stocks of low-grade uranium, officials said Thursday. They said the U.S. troops may have broken U.N. seals meant to keep control of the radioactive material.

http://www.guardian.co.uk/worldlatest/story/0,1280,-2549235,00.html

As time precedes so do the doubts and clarifications. Fox News tends to leap to conclusions and emphasize the WMD possibilities.

# April 11, 2003

"Freedom's untidy, and free people are free to make mistakes and commit crimes and do bad things," Rumsfeld said. "They're also free to live their lives and do wonderful things. And that's what's going to happen here."

> http://www.cnn.com/2003/US/04/11/sprj.irq.pentagon/
> index.html

Rumsfeld is referring in the above comment to all the looting that's occurring right now in Iraq.

The following is Rumsfeld's reply when asked about WMD:

> "We are not going to find them in my view—just as I never believed the inspectors would—by running round seeing if they can open a door and surprise somebody and find something," Rumsfeld said, adding that the focus was on "finding the people" who could help in that effort.
>
> [Same reference as above]

Good Lord! What the hell did we invade the country for if we can't find the reason why we went there (WMD)?

> Mr. Rumsfeld said weapons production facilities needed to "found and secured".

> He warned of a "nexus between terrorist states...and terrorist groups".

The possibility that "some of these weapons could leave the country and [get into] the hands of terrorist networks would be a very unhappy prospect," he said.

Asked at the news conference whether the rationale behind the war required that such banned weapons be found, Donald Rumsfeld said he did he did not "quite get the thrust of the questions", but agreed that "it obviously is important to find them."

http://news.bbc.co.uk/2/hi/middle_east/2933923.stm

I agree, Mr. Rumsfeld, we need to find the WMD.

Washington—Three Iraqi warehouses filled with 2500 barrels of uranium that could be enriched for nuclear weapons—plus radioactive isotopes that could be used for deadly "dirty bombs"—lay unguarded for several days this week as Iraqi mobs swirled around.

http://www.latimes.com/news/nationworld/world/la-war-nuke11apr11004423,1,7121633.stor...

Some people were thinking that this nuclear storage site might be the smoking gun. The UN International Atomic Energy Agency seemed to know about this site and I saw no report of violations. Apparently storage site was sealed shut by UN inspectors.

# April 12, 2003

"We're here for your fucking freedom, so back up right now."

US Marine

Baghdad

CNN, 4:07pm, 04/12/03

Of course, I need to continually remind myself that Marines are not trained as diplomats. The Marines are being asked to perform a disagreeable task under very difficult and unique circumstances.

I'm under the belief that the justification for this war was and still is on very shaky ground. Therefore, I spend a lot of my thoughts and reading about the unfolding story regarding WMD.

> Saddam Hussein's science adviser surrendered to U.S. military authorities Saturday, insisting that Iraq had no weapons of mass destruction and the U.S.-led invasion was unjustified.

> http://www.sfgate.com/cgi-bin/article.cgi?f=/news/archive/2003/04/12/international1034E...

Of course, this adviser may just continue some sort of policy of lying, but possibly he's also telling the truth. I don't see any good reason to lie. He's in U.S. custody.

> Vienna—High levels of radioactivity are normal at Iraq's main nuclear research centre, the UN nuclear agency said Friday, deflating speculation that U.S. Marines might have found new evidence of a weapons program at the site.

http://www.globeandmail.ca/servlet/story/
RTGAM.20030411.wnuk0411/BNStory/Intern.

We continue to find pockets of possible WMD. We find a possible chemical weapon here and there, but we have yet to hear of any confirmed stash of WMD. No laboratory has been found. We found no appearance of any elaborate set of deep underground laboratories and tunnels. I am of the thought that we overestimated Saddam. We put too much belief in our intelligence.

Was an elaborate international conspiracy established to draw the U.S. leadership into a war with Iraq? Certainly among Bin Laden's followers, such a plan would be desirable and fairly easy to implement, if the CIA could be fed false information by double agents. But, I'd like to keep my mind away from such angles because conspiracy theories usually lead to dead ends. However, Saddam Hussein admitted a month before the war started that Iraq no longer possessed WMD. He stated that he felt the need to create an illusion to the rest of the world that he had such weapons in order to deter attacks from his enemies. Now this piece of information comes from my memory. I don't have a reference available. So, two interesting problems exist: People may wish to disagree with me because I can't produce the source of Saddam's statement, and, people may just assume that Saddam is a liar, which immediately implies that he does have WMD.

The President takes the stance that Saddam is a liar. And, indeed, Saddam has lied to the world on multiple occasions, so he can't be trusted. The problem is, however, we haven't found WMD in Iraq during the UN inspection period and after the war started. The place has been scoured for WMD and nothing has been found. So, the President has started a war because he believes Saddam is a liar and the UN inspections can't be trusted, even though Saddam invited the UN into Iraq to look for WMD. Should Bush admit that he made a disastrous mistake?

# April 13, 2003

The contracts for rebuilding Iraq are appearing rather quickly as the war winds down:

- International Resources Group. $70-million contract. This company has four VP's who worked for USAID.

- Bechtel. $700-million contract. Made $770,000 donation to Republicans.

- Washington Group International. Currently bidding for capital reconstruction. Made $438,700 donation to Republicans.

- Halliburton. $500-million contract. Made $700,000 donation to Republicans. Dick Cheney once CEO.

- Flour. Currently bidding for multiple contracts. Made $275,000 donation to Republicans.

One of the chief ideologists behind the war, Richard Perle, yesterday warned that the US would be compelled to act against Syria if it emerged that weapons of mass destruction and been moved there by Saddam's fallen Iraqi regime.

Deputy Defence Secretary Paul Wolfowitz—regarded as the real architect of the Iraqi war and its aftermath—said on Thursday that 'the Syrians have been shipping killers into Iraq to try and kill Americans', adding: 'We need to think about what our policy is towards a country that harbours terrorists or harbours war criminals.'

http://www.observer.co.uk/iraq/story/0,12239,935959,00.
html

Perle and Wolfowitz are clearly dangerous people to listen to. I feel they have very rigid views of the Middle East and believe that America is invincible. Both seem allied with the Likud Party in Israel along with Douglas Feith.

Back to WMD:

> "There are some people who have talked in terms of thousands of tonnes of chemicals and hundreds and hundreds of missiles, and I would say that is way beyond the top end," Sir Alan said, though he added: "I am absolutely convinced that they have got elements of weapons of mass destruction."

http://news.independent.co.uk/world/middle_east/story.
jsp?story=396734

I'm not comforted, Sir Alan, that having "elements" of WMD creates a sufficient reason for war. Also, something must have convinced you, Sir Alan, that these "elements" exist. Could someone absolutely convince me, or the people looking for Iraq's WMD?

The editors of *The Nation* [4/21/2003] propose the following post war steps:

- Humanitarian Aid.
- Insure the troops are thanked and properly cared for.
- Make sure the troops are brought home as soon as possible.
- Make no threats against Iran.
- Insure that we don't take Iraq's oil from its people.
- Work for peace between Palestine and Israel.
- Promote WMD disarmament throughout the Middle East.

To agree with *The Nation* is easy for me. We have destroyed the existing infrastructure in Iraq. The least we can do is fix it. However, I find myself faced with a very difficult problem when asked to deal with repairing extensive physical and social damage without taking the responsibility of government from the people. The Bush Administration proposes a solution that forces "Democracy" on Iraq. What does imposing democracy on a country actually mean? The American story of democracy was not about an invading country imposing our government upon us. Our story involved rebellion from within. Is imposed democracy really, therefore, a democracy? Also, I'm uncomfortable with the phrase *as soon as possible*. When does as-soon-as-possible happen? Today? Next week? Ten years from now?

What about the large amounts of oil in Iraq? Would Americans try to influence the nature of the oil industry in Iraq to model itself after the American style of oil oligarchies: wealth for a few; slavery for the rest? I don't have much confidence that American wisdom will make Iraq a safer, more prosperous place than what she was during Saddam's regime. Vietnam became more prosperous only after the Americans left.

# April 14, 2003

Now Washington is stepping up the rhetoric against Syria. Bush has accused
Syria of starting a WMD program. Of course, WMD seems to be the
prescription to get the Congress to provide the President's war authority. Of
course, we've got Rumsfeld's bluster to help our case:

> Mr. Rumsfeld, who last month accused Syria of channeling
> military equipment including night-vision goggles to Iraq,
> said yesterday: "Being on the terrorist list is not some place
> I'd want to be. The Syrian Government is making a lot of
> bad mistakes, a lot of bad judgment calls, in my view, and
> they're associating with the wrong people."
>
> http://www.timesonline.co.uk/article/0,,5944-645911,00.
> html

Will we ever get rid of this clown? But, what does Lawrence Eagleburger's
comment mean?

> Lawrence Eagleburger, who was US Secretary of State under
> George Bush Snr, told the BBC: "If George Bush [Jnr]
> decided he was going to turn the troops loose on Syria and
> Iran after that he would last in office for about 15 minutes.
> In fact if President Bush were to try that now even I would
> think that he ought to be impeached. You can't get away
> with that sort of thing in this democracy."
>
> http://news.independent.co.uk/world/politics/story.
> jsp?story=397011

Of course, I think bush is heading into trouble over the WMD.

> As Susan Wright, a disarmament expert at the University of Michigan, said last week: "This could be the first war in history that was justified largely by an illusion." Even The Wall Street Journal, one of the administration's biggest cheerleaders, has warned of the "widespread skepticism" the White House can expect if it does not make significant, and undisputed, discoveries of forbidden weapons.

> http://news.independent.co.uk/world/middle_east/story.jsp?story=396733

But, Colin Powell continues to stay the course on WMD:

> "The combat period is over and we can now turn our attention to finding weapons of mass destruction...There's strong evidence and no question about the fact there are weapons of mass destruction," he told BBC television in an interview.

"We will find weapons of mass destruction."

> http://asia.reuters.com/newsArticle.jhtml;jessionid=U5IIIT
> TX1D5ICRBAEKSFFA?type=...

Since Colin Powell destroyed his credibility during his UN presentation, I take his affirmative stance as rather ominous. I can imagine anything happening at this point, if the Administration becomes desperate to retain its power. As Han Blix has speculated, the U.S. could easily plant the evidence it needs. Blix made reference to Powell's report of a nuclear exchange between Niger and Iraq, which turned out to be false. I have already noted how cavalier Powell was when asked about this supposed evidence of WMD. I am suspicious that Powell might be willing to lie and deceive when directed to do so. He's a good soldier.

> Differences have begun to emerge between the US and British governments over the verification of weapons of mass destruction finds.

> Tony Blair said last week that any banned weapons finds would have to be "externally verified", ...

But the US Secretary of State, Colin Powell, repeated yesterday the US view that it was not necessary to involve the United Nations in the search for banned weapons.

http://news.independent.co.uk/world/middle_east/story. jsp?story=397002

I keep realizing the fact that American media is not presenting the brewing controversy over the strangely missing WMD. A question exists over the U.S.'s capability for being objective in this search.

# *April 15, 2003*

I found one of my letters in the SJ Mercury this morning.

Posted on Tue. Apr. 15, 2003

Having won the war, where are we now?

We don't know if Saddam Hussein is alive or dead, but he seems out of the loop. We don't know if weapons of mass destruction exist, but at this point so what? We're close to finishing the war.

Here is what we have accomplished: at least 149 coalition troops dead; thousands of civilians dead; thousands of Iraqi troops dead; hospitals filled with the wounded; the Iraq infrastructure nearly destroyed; and Saddam is missing in action.

Fred Rounds

The irony in this war and wars in the recent past is that the U.S. seems to be the one that either uses WMD or doesn't recognize that we're using such weapons.

The US says it has no plans to remove the debris left over from depleted uranium (DU) weapons it is using in Iraq.

http://news.bbc.co.uk/2/hi/science/nature/2946715.htm

A continuing debate exists over the hazards of depleted uranium (DU). UN reports haven't shown a clear case against

DU, but caution against exposure. I can say that DU adds
nothing to the health value of the environment. DU indeed
carries the potential to make people sick depending on the
level of exposure, especially in places where concentrations of
uranium dust are high, such as where bombs have exploded.
Our arsenal—which we have no compunction in using—
consists of radioactive dirty bombs.

American forces in Iraq say they have discovered 11 mobile
"chemical and biological laboratories" buried in ground near
a factory filled with empty artillery shells.

http://www.timesonline.co.uk/article/0,,5944-647075,00.
html

Apparently these mobile units were found buried, which implies that
they weren't ready for use. I can imagine that using these mobile laboratories
to make weapons grade bio-agents would be very difficult especially in large
quantities. But, the purpose of these trailers needs to be determined.

President George Bush, who faces re-election next year with
two perilous nation-building projects, in Afghanistan and
Iraq, on his hands, is said to have cut off discussion among
his advisers about possibility of taking the "war on terror"
to Syria.

http://www.guardian.co.uk/Iraq/Story/0,2763,937105,00.
html

This decision to stay out of Syria may be a good one for a change.
Wolfowitz, Perle, and Feith appear again to be the voices behind a wider
Middle East war.

United States troops have opened fire on a crowd opposed
to the US-installed governor in the northern Iraqi city of
Mosul, killing at least 10 people and injuring as many as
100, witnesses and doctors said.

http://www.abc.net.au/news/newsitems/s832822.htm

17.8 percent of the Federal budget goes to National Defense: $3790
billion. Perhaps $100-billion would be the bill for Iraq. So, maybe about 6
percent of your taxes go toward this war. I paid about $30,000 in taxes for
2002. So, I suppose I could protest the war by not paying about $1800. Of
course, not paying taxes is illegal and very nasty things can happen to you, if
you decide not to pay. The IRS can attach your wages and assets.

# *April 16, 2003*

What an unmitigated disaster we have dealt the people of Iraq.

> As the flames engulfed Baghdad's National Library, destroying manuscripts many centuries old, the Pentagon admitted that it had been caught unprepared by the widespread looting of antiquities, despite months of warnings from American archaeologists.
>
> http://www.smh.com.au/articles/2003/04/15/1050172600 404.html
>
> Brigadier-General Vince Brooks said US marines and special forces soldiers fired at demonstrators on Tuesday after they came under attack from people shooting guns and throwing rocks.
>
> Http://news.bbc.co.uk/21/hi/middle_east/2951789.stm

The negligent leaders that caused this war travesty should be impeached. No words exist to describe the barbarism that America has so well demonstrated in this slaughter and devastation of the cradle of civilization.

> The 11 cargo containers were filled with new laboratory equipment apparently intended to make conventional weapons, said a team leader Chief Warrant Officer 2 Monte Gonzalez.
>
> http://www.cnn.com/2003/WORLD/meast/0415/sprj.irq. no.labs/index.html

I believe the above article refers to the buried trailers mentioned earlier. The only weapon of mass destruction appears so far to be the American military machine. At this point I don't care whether we find WMD or not. What the world has lost due American "foreign policy" can never be replaced, and the loss can never be justified. And, the Pentagon is sitting around listening to country music.

The burning of the Baghdad National Library reminds me of the history regarding the burning of the libraries at Alexandria, Egypt. Likely Julius Caesar was responsible for this tragedy, but uncertainty exists here. At any rate probably the intellectual works of the ancient world were lost due to the fire. The losses probably included scrolls of Aristotle and Plato. Very likely documents were destroyed that described how the pyramids were built. The world's greatest intellectual records were lost due the ravages of war. Now America can stand with Caesar to claim responsibility for an equal kind of contempt.

# April 17, 2003

I stared at a photo in the *SJ Mercury* today. It was of General Tommy Franks and his staff. They were sitting on ornate couches and chairs in an expansive room within one of Saddam's captured palaces. It seems presumptuous to me when I see our generals occupying the fallen dictator's residence. Looting of the spoils of war occurs to me. The vision of taking liberty of the excesses that belonged to the previous resident presumes that special entitlements go the victor by default. And, I suppose the status of general is necessarily entitled to a palace. But, I find the general's assumption of Saddam's opulence obscene.

> As US secretary of state Colin Powell says: 'The combat period is over, and we can now turn our attention to finding weapons of mass destruction.' ... In short, having won the war, coalition forces now need to justify it.
>
> http://www.spiked-online.com/Articles/00000006DD50. htm
>
> April 16—U.S. officials hope a paper trail will lead them to Iraq's elusive weapons of mass destruction, but coalition forces—and hundreds of looting Iraqis—may have already shredded that path to the so-called smoking gun.
>
> http://abcnews.go.com/sections/world/Primetime/iraq_ WMD030416.html
>
> Why aren't the American people so outraged over being led to war based on an illusion? Why aren't we demanding the evidence immediately?

"This is our American liberation!" spat Ms. Khediary, 70, as she waded through the half-burned books of her second-story library. "I never thought you would do it. I went to the American School. I believed in your moral values. And every night you bombed. Every night, I ran through the streets, an old woman in my nightgown. Look at my library!"

http://www.nytimes.com/2003/04/17/international/worldspecial/17FURY.html

These are the details from ground zero. Often all that we see are the gross results of American troops triumphing over evil. The details create a different picture that involves the death of innocents, the destruction of art, the loss of learning, the obliteration of culture, the disruption of services, and the releasing of criminal inhibitions.

As with this war in which the basis is confused, we end up with people like me who feel the need to say something to those who make decisions for me. A case in point is the City Council of Sunnyvale who recently established a support-the-troops program. The following is the complaint I registered with the Council.

I am disturbed by the Council's action in support of our troops in Iraq. What support-of-our-troops means is not a clearly defined set of actions or beliefs. The Council did not consider any resolution regarding its position on the war and/or the attendant foreign policy, so any sort of symbolic gesture in the name of the American troops contains no inherent or accepted meaning. Since I find this war not only offensive to my sense of justice, but also illegal within the confines of the UN charter, I would find any display of yellow ribbons and such to be just a symbol of the offense we have committed. I would ask that you reconsider your actions regarding the support of our troops. I would wait until the basis for this war [weapons of mass destruction] plays out. Also, our troops have killed civilians. I wonder if you support that kind of activity.

I guess this letter is an example of me acting locally, but thinking globally. Many local governments, especially here in California are taking a stance against the war. *Support-the-troops* for many of the antiwar population means bring our military home and let's not fight this war.

> Distraught soldiers were saying: 'I ain't prepared for this, I didn't come here to shoot civilians. 'The colonel countered that the Iraqis were using inhabitants to kill marines, that 'soldiers were being disguised as civilians, and that ambulances were perpetrating terrorist attacks.'

http://www.counterpunch.org/guerrin04162003.html

The soldier killed a civilian. The commanding officer assures the troops that the killing is O.K.

# April 18, 2003

Quote from the Chairman of the Joint Chiefs:

> "Some are going to recover very quickly; others are going to have to live with their injuries for the rest of their lives,' Myers said. "They'll never escape the pain in some cases or, perhaps, regain lost opportunities this conflict has brought them."

> http://apnews.excite.com/article/20030417/D7QFG6080. html

General Myers is speaking about the 475 wounded Americans. He is speaking about his own troops. I think he realizes the tragedy that has happened because of this war, but I wonder if he realizes his culpability in complying with orders from Bush. He apparently didn't question the reasons for this war or its legality. We can often accept loss in wars in which we are defending ourselves against invasion. But, Iraq clearly wasn't invading, nor was she collecting WMD. We are only now trying to justify this war by frantically searching for the "smoking gun." Wars can only be prosecuted by those willing to fight them. General Myers is certainly compelled to follow orders from the Commander in Chief. But, where are the limits in following orders? Generals can ask questions and wonder why his or her country needs to go off to war. Generals can also have a sense of values that require moral certainty that his/her orders are compliant with those values. Of course, a value of moral certainty carries a cost, which could mean careers being lost.

> "I don't think we'll discover anything, myself," Rumsfeld said at a town hall-style with Pentagon employees.

http://apnews.excite.com/article/20030417/D7QFG6080.
html

Then why look, Mr. Rumsfeld? With all the reward money flying about for people who can show the way to the door in front of the WMD, we ought to be able to find it. Apparently, the senior Iraq leadership doesn't know where the WMD is.

> April 17—When two former Iraqi regime leaders surrendered to U.S. authorities early this week, coalition officials anticipated uncovering a treasure trove of intelligence on Iraq's weapons of mass destruction program. ABCNEWS has learned, however, that the two men, who were privy to critical details about Iraq's WMD development and capability, have not provided the smoking gun investigators hoped for.

> http://www.abcnews.go.com/sections/us/DailyNews/
> ITeamInsider.html

I wonder if anybody really cares at this point that we were led into this war based on a false premise. Maybe we haven't evolved much beyond the spectators who would picnic along the edges of the battlefield while American Civil War soldiers fought each other. Is the unfolding tragedy just another form of entertainment?

> Fresh information has emerged of banking scandals involving the family of the Pentagon's preferred candidate to shape post-war Iraq, Ahmad Chalabi.

> http://www.smh.com.au/articles/2003/04/17/1050172708
> 630.html

I wonder if Chalabi is a friend of Niel Bush. I find it very ironic that the Pentagon would want a bank criminal to help lead Iraq.

# *April 20, 2003*

Tomorrow I shall be going down to Mexico for a mission trip with the Church. I won't be keeping daily notes in the journal. The rest is welcome, however. I need to separate myself from the daily flood of bad news. When living with the inhabitants of the Mexican border, I find no better way to feel isolated. There are no TV's or newspapers.

In the meantime the U.S. is still looking for the reason behind going to Iraq. We still have found nothing. I am seeing more people and journalists asking questions about where the weapons are that drove us to war. Many are concerned that if we don't find these weapons, American credibility in the world will be hopelessly damaged. I wonder why no one is demanding that the President either present the weapons or admit they don't exist. An admission of such failure would probably lead to the President leaving office either voluntarily or through impeachment.

Apparently some Congresspeople are demanding WMD accountability from the President, but little public note is being made of these demands. I can see the American attention start to divert as the war draws to a close. The demise of Laci Peterson has replaced Iraq as the lead story, especially on Fox News. Maybe the President will get away with destroying a sovereign nation for no good reason.

Not everybody agrees with my perspective. Ms. X [Name changed] sees fit to reply to one of my letters to the SJ Mercury:

> Ignoring the obvious
>
> Fred Rounds and Mr. Y [Name Changed] must have blinders on ("Have won the war, where are we now? Letters, April 15).

First, Mr. Rounds neglected to mention a few other accomplishments of the U.S. in Iraq. How about the liberation of 35 million people? How about the end of murdering, torturing, oppressive regime?

Ms. X

SJ Mercury

I don't want to exclude or deny Ms. X's feelings. The letter to the editor probably isn't the best forum to exchange ideas, but this venue does bring to the fore the varying viewpoints on this war. Actually I believe Ms. X and I could find common ground on the subject of liberation and public safety. We could debate the war, however, as a means to a political end.

# *April 28, 2003*

I've returned from the mission trip to Tijuana. During the last week I received no news: no TV, newspapers, Internet, or radio. My focus was on the families that lived in a small community called El Pipila. I worked primarily on putting electrical wiring in a makeshift house occupied by a woman named Magdalena. She had five kids and an alcoholic husband who regularly abuses is wife and children.

The local Pastor of the Iglesia Presbiteriana wanted to supply electricity to Magdalena's house, and she had been praying for this gift as well. I guess I came to answer her prayers, but I'm not sure of the value of my gift. Magdelena doesn't buy electricity. She takes the power by tapping into the source surreptitiously. So, perhaps I deepened the extent of the "crime." I also potentially increased her dependence on the electrical culture. I've never done a project in Mexico in which I've left feeling completely convinced that I've done a good thing for humanity. I've made life more comfortable for some, but I've also created greater potential for pollution and environment waste. And, the Mexican/U.S. border seems to be a catch point for American waste and damage.

The Americans who traveled with me were young: 13 up to around 26. Most seemed to be the cream of the white American family. All of them were smart in school, well poised around adults, serious, and "good" Christians. Many had already traveled around the world to places such as Africa and China. I knew that I was with a very special group of people: people of privilege, advantages, and worldly exposure at an early age.

What will these people turn into? Will the world be a good place for these young people to work? Will a place exist for them to thrive?

I didn't lose much information during the week away from the Iraq war. No WMD has been found even though potential unconventional weapons seem to come and go daily. Ninety sites have been examined with no positive findings. The search has been disorganized with one team making a find and then filing a news report. Then another team counters the same find and then files a counter-news report.

> "Think of scenes we've all witnessed – free Iraqis pulling down a statue of Saddam Hussein, embracing coalition forces and celebrating their newfound freedom," Mr. Rumsfeld said.

> "It will certainly take its place alongside the Berlin Wall, the liberation of Paris.

> http://www.abc.net.au/news/justin/nat/newssnat-28apr2003-83.htm

So far without the discovery of the reason behind this war, I see this American military action as one of the greatest debacles in history. It ranks with Hitler's seizure of Paris.

# April 29, 2003

U.S. troops opened fire on a group of Iraqi demonstrators near Baghdad yesterday, killing at least 13 people and wounding 75 others, according to reports from the area.

http://www.guardian.co.uk/Iraq/Story/0,2763,945719,00.html

Saddam Hussein was intolerant of dissent. He opposed any sort of protest with abuse, such as physical punishment, or imprisonment. How much of the same sort of repression are we providing? We're installing our own hand-picked government. We're killing people in the streets. We're imprisoning Iraqis who decide to create government authority for their local communities. I wouldn't be at all surprised if our intelligence efforts consisted of various types of abuses and torture.

I don't like bullies, but bullies seem to rule the world on the backs of all of us. If the people don't cooperate with bullies, the bullies will just hit harder. The strategy to influence a bully is persistent non-cooperation on a large scale (Gandhi ). But, some will die as a consequence of resistance.

# April 30, 2003

US troops today opened fire on Iraqi civilians for the second time this week as an angry crowd in Falluja protested over an earlier shooting.

http://www.guardian.co.uk/Iraq/Story/0,2763,946651,00.html

For a second day in a row we've killed civilians in a crowd. These civilians were apparently protesting the U.S. shooting that occurred yesterday.

This Thursday Bush will declare the war officially over. However, the weapons of mass destruction still haven't been found. All the people in custody who apparently know about these weapons claim Iraq simply doesn't have WMD anymore. Even though rewards are available, no one has come forward with definitive information. Clearly a lot of people would have been involved in moving, destroying, and developing the apparently large quantities of weapons that the U.S. claims Iraq has. Not one person, however, has pointed to any stash of WMD. I'm under the impression that no weapons exist. Colin Powell talks about nuggets of evidence arriving everyday that when put together will ultimately build the story of what happened to the WMD. Unfortunately these nuggets aren't helping to reveal the danger that led to this war.

We can all see the damage control that the Administration is now involved in. We keep hearing encouragement that we'll find the WMD. But, we also see interest waning in this war.

# May 1, 2003

The U.S. military shot two more protestors yesterday.

> Lt. Col. Tobin Green of the 3rd Armored Cavalry Regiment said the shootings were the result of "the evildoers ... deliberately placing at risk all of the good civilians."

> http://www.bayarea.com/mld/mercurynews/news/speacial_packages/iraq/5754661.htm

I feel comfortable knowing that our military leaders are rooting out the evil doers by indiscriminately shooting into crowds of people.

> Seven US soldier were today wounded in a grenade attack on their base in the Iraqi city of Falluja, where troops have killed at least 15 civilians during protests this week.

> http://www.guardian.co.uk/Iraq/Story/0,2763.947229,00. html

> "In Iraq, we were dealing with an army, as opposed to a terrorist situation," Rumsfeld said.

> Http://www.guardian.co.uk/worldlatest/story/0,1280,-2628540,00.html

I wonder who threw the grenades at the Americans. Were they an army or terrorists?

> Washington—High ranking Iraqi prisoners are uniformly denying Saddam Hussein's government had any weapons of mass destruction before the war, U.S. officials familiar with their interrogations said Tuesday.

http://www.bayarea.com/mld/mercurynews/news/special_
packages/iraq/5750165.htm

President George Bush's National Security Adviser, Condoleezza Rice, is now acknowledging that Iraq's weapons of mass destruction program is less clear-cut, and probably more difficult to establish, than the White House portrayed before the war.

http://www.smh.com.au/articles/2003/04/30/1051381997
497.html

"We were not lying," one administration official told ABC News on Friday. "But it was just a matter of emphasis." No, it wasn't. Iraq's possession of weapons of mass destruction is central to the legitimacy of the war.

http://www.latimes.com/la-ed-wmd29apr29,0,3138181.
story

Everyday the state of the WMD in Iraq becomes clearer. We don't have a clue what exists or doesn't exist. To say WMD was hidden in dual function factories is another smokescreen that will always remain ambiguous. Bush was clear about the quantities of Anthrax and chemical weapons Iraq hadn't accounted for. We went to war to eliminate Saddam's arsenal of WMD. This story won't change.

# May 2, 2003

Bush sauntered aboard the Aircraft Carrier *Abraham Lincoln* sporting a flight suit and survival vest. He then commenced to diminish the importance of WMD in his speech while emphasizing the mysterious connection between Saddam and Bin Laden. In fact, no relationship seems to exist at all. Bush pronounced that the U.S. has collected "hundreds of sites" that hold potential for containing WMD. He may be referring to approximately 150 known sites of which 90 have been checked with zero discoveries.

The tragedy is that America is buying the Bush choreography. Seventy-one percent of polled Americans think Bush is doing a great job. Unfortunately no one has come forward to counter the baby food spewing form Bush's mouth. I think we all realize now that UN inspection teams were doing a good job, and if we had continued this process, we would have been successful in determining whether Saddam had a functional WMD arsenal.

Now America has a hero for a President. We don't seem to care about what we've done to Iraq. We don't care about the people we've killed, or the terrible loss in Iraq's treasures. We only see the mindless image of a President strutting across the deck of an aircraft carrier. He holds the first two fingers of his hand up in a peace sign. How many people are confused by this mixed signal of a peace sign from a man in military combat garb?

> With new tactics and precision weapons, we can achieve military objectives without violence against civilians.
>
> President Bush speaking aboard USS Abraham Lincoln.
>
> http://www.bayarea.com/mld/mercurynews/5767533.htm

I'm sure the twelve-year-old Iraqi boy who lost his arms to American bombs appreciates knowing the precision of our weapons.

> And anyone in the world, including the Arab world, who works and sacrifices for freedom has a loyal friend in the United States of America.

President Bush, same speech as documented above.

Let's see who our loyal friends are:

France?    No.
Russia?    No.
Germany? No.
Canada?    No.
Mexico?    No.
China?    No.

The national unemployment is now about 6%--the worst since 1994. Silicon Valley's unemployment may be as high as 10%. Gross domestic product growth for last quarter was around 1.6%. This rate isn't fast enough to support job growth, so we'll probably see more unemployment in the future.

Bush wants to reduce taxes to stimulate the economy. First, this action means nothing to the already unemployed. In addition, for most tax payers the tax reduction doesn't provide enough money to make more purchases in the market. Essentially the tax reduction merely increases the deficit. Federal dollars go into paying interest, which doesn't benefit anyone, except the country that makes the loan: China, for example. And, the war produces no return on investment, so we see no stimulus; rather, we see further loss. So how can a tax reduction do much good for anyone?

# May 3, 2003

This is the statement Powell made in February, 2003 justifying the need for UN action in Iraq.

> "EVERY STATEMENT I make today are backed up by sources, solid sources," Powell said. "These are not assertions."

> http://www.msnbc.com/news/908088.asp

Well, Mr. Powell, I would wonder how solid those sources are at this point. Where's the WMD?

If you review my notes on April 17, 2003, you'll see a letter I sent to the Sunnyvale City Council. The following is the reply I got 13 days later from Councilman Jim Walker:

> Mr. Rounds,
>
> I'm just reviewing some old emails and I came across your feedback once again. As was clearly stated at the meeting, the Sunnyvale City Council took no position on the validity or legality of the Iraq war. Frankly, the City has no more insight on the war than what you or I read in the paper and that is certainly insufficient to adopt any reasonable policy position. We believe that the City should only weigh in on issues of specific concerns to the city that we have significant expertise on. The fact that some of our residents and family members have been deployed does impact us directly and it is appropriate for the City to place yellow ribbons in support of the safe return of our enlisted men.

Our goal with the Yellow Ribbons is to show support to those who, through no fault of their own, have loved ones at risk. It is a trying time for them, many who are in complete opposition to our involvement in Iraq. You, on the other hand, would offer nothing to help their pain and suffering. You can only see your narrow political interests.

What ever your opinions concerning this conflict, you can not hold the troops or their relatives personally responsible for decisions made by elected officials in Washington. You suggest that we not support the safe return of our troops. I find that harsh and unreasonable. We can not blame the failure of foreign policy on friends and relatives placed in harm's way by those policy decisions. That's a ludicrous position to take. Your anger is clearly misplaced.

Your lack of compassion suggests that you are no different than those in the Whitehouse. How sad for you.

Jack Walker

Councilmember

City of Sunnyvale

At least Mr. Walker doesn't worry about choosing the most politic response to one of his constituents.

# May 4, 2003

"I feel like I've fulfilled something," he said after returning to camp. "I feel like I've done something very good. At least there's a shining gem in the middle of this devastation, and maybe these people will remember that Americans did something good."

SSGT James Mattwig
U.S. Army, Baghdad
SJ Mercury, 5/4/03

The quote above expresses the feeling of SSGT James Mattwig as he helped save the sight of a young Iraqi girl who suffered blindness due to glass shrapnel that entered her left eye.

This one quote describes a great deal about war: the cruelty, devastation, deprivation, and the loss of certainty regarding moral values. The opportunity to show humanity to someone in need becomes so rare that the memory stands out as a "shining gem."

Then we have the President's poisonous, hate-filled remarks to compare with the soldier on the ground:

"We're learning that Tariq Aziz still doesn't know how to tell the truth," Bush told the reporters outside his Crawford ranch. "He didn't know how to tell the truth when he was in office. He doesn't know how to tell the truth" when he's been a captive.

G.W. Bush
SJ Mercury
5/4/03

Considering all that's been said leading up to this war, I'd say Bush and Aziz are a lot alike. Bush has difficulty telling the truth because he doesn't know what the truth is. I'm still waiting to see what happened to the WMD, which Aziz has claimed repeatedly no longer exists.

> As the search goes on without bearing fruit, doubts are spreading. "It's hard to believe that we won't eventually find some poison gas or crude biological weapons," columnist Paul Krugman wrote in The New York Times last week. "But those aren't true WMDs ... One wonders whether most of the public will ever learn that the original case for war has turned out to be false."

> http://news.independent.co.uk/world/middle_east/story. jsp?story=402969

I wonder whether the public will learn that the reason for this war was based on a false premise. I think the case for WMD has already been forgotten and not much effort exists to hold anyone accountable for the crime we've committed. As a matter of fact, I don't think anyone will label our deed in Iraq a crime. It will be a glorious victory for America. The history of what got us to Iraq will certainly be recorded, but people will go on with their lives. This war did not affect the American people enough to spur a convincing level of dissent. Americans got truly upset about Vietnam only after tens of thousands of Americans had died. I think we can see now what Americans will support from their government:

small wars,
unilateralism,
preemption,
deception,
cronyism.

We should learn just to expect these behaviors from our government. I'm not sure our elected leaders intentionally try to be dishonest or deceptive. I think conditions and circumstances force people into situations which become quagmires. To think that Bush merely sees an opportunity to enrich his friends with war contracts and oil deals is a very cynical place to put the mind.

# May 5, 2003

On March 17, Bush said:

> "Intelligence gathered by this and other governments leaves no doubt that the Iraqi regime continues to possess and conceal some of the most lethal weapons ever devised.

> "This regime has already used weapons of mass destruction against Iraq's neighbors and against Iraq's people. The regime has a history of reckless aggression in the Middle East. It has a deep hatred of America and our friends. And it has aided, trained and harbored terrorists, including operatives of al-Qaida.

> "The danger is clear. Using chemical, biological or – one day – nuclear weapons obtained with the help of Iraq, the terrorists could fulfill their stated ambitions and kill thousands or hundreds of thousands of innocent people, in our country or any other."

> http://www.newsday.com/news/nationworld/world/ny-wob ush04326785may04,0,2877938.st...

With 78% of the American people supporting the war, I guess the exaggeration that got us there doesn't make much difference.

Apparently Huda Salih Mahdi Ammash—Mrs. Anthrax—has been taken into custody. She is supposed to have detailed understanding of Iraq's bio-weapons program. She denies she had much to do with it. I expect this capture will reveal nothing.

Rumsfeld keeps opening his mouth.  In the following he quotes Al Capone.

"You'll get more with a kind word and a gun than a kind word alone."

The tragedy is that Secretary Rumsfeld believes the garbage that he spews out.

The following is a story excerpt by Paul Street, May 4, 2003.  I question its truth, but I would indeed want such an act investigated.

> Eyewitnesses report that Americans had been keeping the streets in front of the museum clear with gunfire, prior to the looting.  Then an American tank pulled up in front of the Museum and fired into it, producing a hole that was too high to have been made by looters.  US soldiers murdered the guards in front of the Museum's administrative building and told US Arabic translators to direct looters to enter.  After that it was off to the National Archives, where millions of pages of historical material were burned by mobs under the approving eye of the US military.
>
> http://www.zmag.org/content/showarticle.cfm?SectionID=36&ItemID=3572

The Washington Times tells the same story as above but from the perspective of the US soldiers who were present.  The tank apparently did shoot a hole above the door and possibly killed some people in the process.  However, the act of encouraging looters is not confirmed.

# May 6, 2003

This is the way the war ends:   not with the jubilation of
the liberated but with the whimpering of ragged children.
"Water! Water!" they cry, running from the roadside towards
passing cars, thrusting their fingers towards their mouths in
the salute of the thirsty.

http://www.theage.com.au/articles/2003/05/04/10598760
4147.html

The above is a story about Uum Qasr, Iraq, the first city "liberated" in
the war.  This location is also the seaport used to bring in supplies for the
military and humanitarian efforts.  It is the first report that I've read that also
describes a growing humanitarian shortfall.

The human effects of war are often neglected, since the victor gains
the spoils and glory on the heads of the vanquished.  The innocent civilian
becomes a residual that often gets abandoned after the war machine departs
the area.

The White House is refusing to release for national security reasons a 900-page
Congressional report about 9/11.  The Administration feels that the data must be
classified, even though much of the information has already been published on
the Internet, such as the well-known FBI warning that al-Qaeda supporters were
training at U.S. flight schools.  And, the report does insinuate that the President
and the National Security Adviser received warnings of possible terrorist attacks
before 9/11.  We even had one potential hijacker, Zachiarias Mussoui, in custody.
Perhaps some of the information might embarrass the White House.  Yet, I don't
think the White House gets embarrassed.

# May 7, 2003

Ex-Senator Bob Kerrey said:

> "It was the weakest and most misleading argument we could use." Kerrey added, "It appears that they have the intelligence. The problem is, they didn't like the conclusions."

> http://www.newyorker.com/fact/content/?030512fa_fact

This comment involved the collection of manipulated intelligence that justified the Iraq war. Most of the intelligence was obtained from exiles whose testimony often proved to be false or outdated.

Reports are appearing today of a discovery of a mobile bio-weapons laboratory. Of course, its purpose is completely inconclusive.

> Villagers surrounding the Tuwaitha facility, about six miles (10 kilometers) south of Baghdad, said they used drums from the site to hold water, dumping material from the drums on the ground before using them. Scientists said the drums contained uranium oxide, or yellowcake.

> http://www.cnn.com/2003/WORLD/meast/05/07/sprj.irq.main/index.html

Wonderful! I thought we were guarding this facility.

> "Inspectors only left Baghdad a few days before the start of the campaign," Wallace said. "Because they were so clever in disguising them and burying them so deep, they themselves had a problem getting to it."

http://www.guardian.co.uk/worldlatest/
story/0,1280,-2650402,00.html

I believe General Wallace is really saying, "I don't know where the hell the WMD are."

> Earlier Wednesday, Lt. Gen. William Wallace said that American forces have collected "plenty of documentary evidence" suggesting that Saddam had an active program for weapons of mass destruction.
>
> [Same reference as above]

But, why doesn't the documentary evidence show where the WMD is?

> "The NBC (nuclear, biological, chemical) operations are being looked at as more important..., but they're not the main priority, which is establishing security," said Captain Bobbie Jackson, chemicals officer for the division's 2$^{nd}$ Brigade, according to AFP. "Once all the pockets of resistance are cleared up I think the search will intensify."
>
> http://www.albawaba.com/news/index.php3?sid=248773&
> lang=je&dir=news

Woops! The generals might need to shut their captains up, since we might get the impression that finding the reason for the war is not an important mission. After all, terrorists might get their hands on these weapons and then where'd we be. However, I can see the Captain's point of view: searching for hidden weapons may be pretty hard with bullets flying around.

> But, where the hell is the:
>
> 25,000 liters of Anthrax,
>
> 38,000 liters of botulinum toxin,
>
> 500 tons of Sarin, Mustard, VX,
>
> 29,984 prohibited munitions?

# May 8, 2003

> Washington—Halliburton Co.'s emergency, no-bid contract to work on Iraq's oil wells must be fully disclosed, a Democratic lawmaker says, pointing to the Army's admission that the company has a far more lucrative role than originally believed.

> http://www.suntimes.com/output/iraq/halli07.html

Basically what we've got with Halliburton is a sole source contract based on the assertion that Halliburton owns the only skill to revitalize the oil industry in Iraq. I am surprised that no one has protested the award of this contract. But, apparently Halliburton does have the only unique skills for large-scale oil projects. Frankly this award is a little convenient under the circumstances. Vice President Dick Cheney was the CEO of Halliburton, and apparently he still has some company holdings in a blind trust. He declares, however, that he sold off all his holdings. Whatever the situation is, I smell the stink of cronyism.

> A severe shortage of clean drinking water has left southern Iraq facing a mass cholera outbreak, the World Health Organization warned today.

> http://www.guardian.co.uk/Iraq/Story/0,2763,951853,00.html

We've wreaked havoc on Iraq and the humanitarian issues seem to be moving faster than we're able to keep up. What seems to be happening is the same as the last Gulf war: more indirect civilian consequences than direct damage through military weapons.

Bagdad, Iraq, May 7 –Hundreds of Iraqi doctors, nurses, and health workers demonstrated today against a decision by the American authorities here to appoint Ali al-Janabi, senior Baath Party member, to be minister of health.

http://www.nytimes.com/2003/05/08/international/worldspecial/08BAAT.html

Did the U.S. buy out the Baath Party to make the invasion of Baghdad easier? The trade could have led to money and retention of some power. Who knows?

# May 9, 2003

The United States Army commander in Iraq has said that while there is documentary evidence to suggest that the country had an active program for chemical and biological weapons, nothing has been found to show the country's military was prepared to use them on US forces.

http://www.smh.com.au/articles/2003/05/08/1052280379 817.html

What was the terrible hurry to go after Iraq's supposed WMD? We were so concerned about terrorists getting their hands on them. Now we haven't found any WMD and we aren't looking that hard. We have heard that around 600 potential WMD sites exist. We've looked at maybe 100 of them. All we have to show for the effort is a very clean truck that some are saying is a mobile bio-weapons lab.

Yet, under our watch actual nuclear waste has disappeared. Somehow we stopped caring about the threat of WMD and we moved on to other matters of perhaps more interest.

UNITED NATIONS, May 8 — A draft resolution to be introduced by the United States, Britain and Spain on Friday morning lifting economic sanctions against Iraq calls for the Security Council to endorse American and British control of Iraq's political development and financial resources for at least 12 months.

Under the resolution, new Iraqi oil revenues and at least $3 billion in the current United Nations-controlled escrow fund would be transferred to a new Iraqi Assistance Fund to be "disbursed at the direction of" the United States and Britain — referred to as the "provisional authority" — in consultation with the interim government to be formed in Iraq.

http://www.nytimes.com/2003/05/09/international/ worldspecial/09DIPL.html

Note the word *oil* is buried in the above article. The oil revenues will be managed by the U.S.-led coalition. But more, the National Central Bank of Iraq will be managed by an ex-CEO of Bank of America. Everything now comes together in a nice package. WMD was our excuse and oil was our desire.

Of course, 2004 is fast approaching, and some cats are still in the bag that could cause some trouble.

…Newsweek has learned, President Bush's chief lawyer has privately signaled that the White House may seek to invoke executive privilege over key documents relating to the attacks [9/11] in order to keep them out of the hands of investigators for the National Commission on Terror Attacks Upon the United States—the independent panel created by Congress to probe all aspects of 9-11.

http://www.msnbc.com/news/910676.asp

The White House doesn't want the 9/11 story to get too detailed. The 9/11 story is dangerous in that if any allusion arises that the White House might have been negligent, then votes may be lost.

# May 10, 2003

> . . .Donald Rumsfeld, sat on the board of a company that three years ago sold two light water nuclear reactors to North Korea – a country he now regards as part of the "axis of evil" and which has been targeted for regime change by Washington because of its efforts to build nuclear weapons.
>
> http://www.smh.com.au/articles/2003/05/09/1052280441337.html

Rumsfeld's company is based in Zurich. Of course, the objective of the sale was to make money. Treaties be damned. If the American values aren't profitable, then why not work for a non-American company. Rumsfeld and Cheney have always had questionable business ethics.

> Iraqis on Friday welcomed U.S. and British moves to lift U.N. economic sanctions but called for the United Nations or an Iraqi interim government to take charge of the nation's oil wealth, not Washington.
>
> http://www.reuters.com/newsArticle.jhtml

Sorry, my Iraqi friends, but American democracy doesn't work that way. You'll eventually get a chance to vote for the candidate of our choice.

> The U.S. found another mobile biology laboratory [ http://www.iht.com/articles/95847.html ]. This lab had been looted. Al Gore had noted not long ago that a war in Iraq would potentially cause the WMD to be spread to the terrorists. So far, the conditions have appeared ideal for Gore's prediction to come true.

# May 11, 2003

Bremer's appointment and Bodine's departure are occurring as concern grows in Washington and foreign capitals about the pace of the U.S. reconstruction program in Iraq. Several people involved in the process have said Garner and his staff—as well as his superiors at the Pentagon – did not properly plan for the task, from repairing damage suffered during the war to restarting government ministries and forming an Iraqi-led interim administration.

http://www.washingtonpost.com/wp-dyn/articles/A40210-2003May10.html

Apparently we're not satisfied with our current cleaning service, so we're replacing it. The problem is we've got a pretty big mess to clean up. The fact that war creates a mess seems to be a surprise to the Administration.

Also, now that we've determined that WMD is not such a big deal, the search team is leaving.

The group directing all known U.S. search efforts for weapons of mass destruction in Iraq is winding down operations without finding proof that President Saddam Hussein kept clandestine stocks of outlawed arms, according to participants.

http://www.washingtonpost.com/wp-dyn/articles/A40212-2003May10.html

The American people don't seem terribly concerned over the news that the search is winding down. Apparently a group of about 2000 WMD experts are organizing to continue the search, but what I'm seeing is a group that will be sifting through all the remaining sites and existing documentation. The mission is to piece together a believable story of what happened to the WMD, so as to rescue the President from a credibility issue during the 2004 election.

I'm reading many articles about our failure to achieve credibility in the WMD pursuit. I find the story at http://www.observer.co.uk/international/story/0,6903,953497,00.html to be particularly revealing. I outline this articles points:

- Colin Powell singled out Taji, Iraq as the place that "housed chemical weapons." Yet, a thorough search of Taji has turned up nothing.

- The U.S. has 2600 people in Iraq now looking for WMD. 110 sites have been searched. Nothing has been found. Suspected discoveries have turned out to be benign.

- Because of Rumsfeld's disappointment with the CIA's inability to find conclusive evidence of WMD, the Defense Department set up a "cabal" of about twelve analysts to develop arguments based on existing intelligence. The cabal reports to Paul Wolfowitz.

- The cabal created a doomsday scenario involving Iraq's WMD. Tony Blair announced that Iraq could produce chemical and biological weapons in just 45 minutes.

- The question is asked whether the weapons could be hidden.

- No weapons have been found in Tikrit, Saddam's birthplace.

- Looters could have taken the weapons. Such a prospect creates a chilling scenario if WMD ends up in a black market.

- A "massive picture of intelligence misuse has emerged." Blair's intelligence dossier turned out to be plagiarism. The nuclear fuel transaction with Niger turned out to be false.

- Iraqi defectors testimony has been misused. Only part of Kamel's testimony was presented, completely eliminating the fact that Kamel ordered Iraq's WMD stocks to be destroyed.

- Virtually all the captured WMD experts have declared unanimously that Iraq has no WMD.

- The only concrete evidence so far are two trucks set up with biological production and testing equipment.

# May 12, 2003

"In Iraq there were no drugs until March 2003," said Salah Sha'amikh, a pharmacist. "You would be hanged for trafficking. But now you can get heroin, cocaine, anything." He pulled out a Russian-made 8.5mm pistol which he says he keeps to protect his wares.

http://news.independent.co.uk/world/middle_east/story. jsp?story=405125

According to the story above Baghdad has picked up some of the habits of large American cities, drugs in particular. Saddam was able to keep drugs out of the city by using harsh threats and punishment.

The Shia ayatollah whose return from a 23-year exile has drawn huge crowds across southern Iraq demanded yesterday that US-led forces should leave the country.

http://www.timesonline.co.uk/article/0,,5944-677543,00. html

We may want freedom and democracy, but a powerful majority of Shi'ites may win an election. Iraq's government may converge to a theocracy—Iran style.

# May 13, 2003

I heard Senator Feingold ( D – Wisconsin ) speaking this morning about the President's policies toward terrorism. He is deeply critical of what appears as a severe lack in consistency regarding the U.S. efforts against terrorism, especially with regard to the war in Iraq, which Feingold claims is a major diversion from the war on terrorism, since no relationship exists between 9/11 and Saddam.

Feingold deliberately asks the question concerning the whereabouts of WMD. He made two points:

1. Either our intelligence was wrong to begin with, or;
2. The weapons have disappeared which creates a serious concern that perhaps terrorists purloined them.

Feingold creates the logical conditions that the President needs to answer to, but the questions are nothing new and the President hasn't responded to the "terrible" risks that he so carefully laid out before the war's start.

> Over a month after the end of hostilities launched by President Bush to find and destroy Iraqi weapons of mass destruction, U.S. military teams have found little to justify the administration's claim that Iraq was concealing vast stocks of chemical and biological agents and was actively working on a covert nuclear weapons program.
>
> http://story.news.yahoo.com/news...5/13/03

The questions are on the table, but the voices asking them are not particularly loud. I feel our Senators should be demanding to know where the weapons are and why we went into this war.

Of course, Democratic Presidential candidate, Senator Bob Graham, is trying hard to cast some aspersions toward the President.

> Sen. Bob Graham on Sunday accused the Bush Administration of engaging in a "coverup" of intelligence failures before and after Sept. 11 attacks to shield it from embarrassment, and said the war with Iraq has allowed al-Qaida and other terrorist groups to become a greater threat to Americans than ever before.
>
> http://www.latimes.com/la-na-graham12may12,0,100697.
> story

I doubt strongly that Graham will pull a Daniel-Ellsberg style of revelation. Unfortunately, however, a revelation from a disenchanted citizen may again be what we all need at this point.

In the meantime terrorist attacks continue.

> More than 90 people, including 10 to 12 US citizens, were killed in suicide bombings that rocked three expatriate housing compounds in Saudi Arabia, State Department officials said Tuesday.
>
> http://story.news.yahoo.com/news?tmpl=story&cid=1515&
> ncid=1515&e=1&u=/afp/200305...

Attacking Iraq has had no effect on abating the terrorist threat. The terrorism described above coincided with Colin Powell's scheduled trip to Saudi Arabia.

# May 14, 2003

The *SJ Mercury News* was interesting this morning. Apparently the new American interim authority, Paul Bremer, has directed the U.S. military to shoot looters on site. As unnamed official said:

> "They are going to start shooting a few looters so that the word gets around…"
>
> *SJ Mercury*, 5.15.03

On Fox News about 7:30am this morning, I saw a video taken from a news vehicle driving down a Baghdad street. The scene was men, women, and children looting. Entire families were pushing stolen cars down the street. Children carried televisions. A man walked off with an air conditioner. The looting was so blatant that no one felt the need to be concerned about getting caught. Many of the looters waved at the news camera. I can't imagine shooting any of these people.

Of course, Major General Buford Blount admitted later [www.guardian. co.uk/worldlatest/story/0,1280,-2675843,00.html] that the military will not shoot unless threatened with weapons. The decision of threat will be up to the soldier.

So, what I seem to be experiencing with this looting story is news that appears from an unknown official who declares an extravagant proclamation only to be later tempered by someone with a name.

> U.S. officials said the ceasefire with the Mujahadeen Khalq could be the first step in an arrangement to provide safe haven for the leadership of the Iranian opposition, which

appears on the State Department list of terrorist groups. Iran has demanded the extradition of the Mujahadeen leadership.

http://216.239.41.100/search?q=cache:3obc_OvJdSkJ:216. 26.163.62/2003/ss_iraq_04_24.ht...

Excuse me, I'm all for peaceful solutions, but isn't protecting these "terrorists" the kind of thing we did with Saddam and Osama Bin Laden in years past.

> Britain back-tracked on the contentious issue of Iraqi weapons of mass destruction yesterday when the foreign secretary, Jack Straw, was forced to concede that hard evidence might never be uncovered.

> http://www.guardian.co.uk/Iraq/Story/0,2763,956262,00. html

Jack, what happened to the 10,000 liters of Anthrax? What happened to Iraq's ability to weaponize WMD in 45 minutes? Jack, either you've exaggerated the threat, intelligence was way off the mark, the weapons have been looted or lost, or Iraq told us the truth that WMD no longer existed. But, the truth is, Jack, you don't know, and I don't think you really ever knew.

> An Army general in northern Iraq said today that Saddam Hussein's government might have destroyed stocks of chemical weapons some time before the United States attacked Iraq to topple Mr. Hussein.

> But Maj. Gen. David H. Petraeus, command of the 101st Airborne Division, said it was still too early to determine definitively the location or status of Iraq's suspected arsenal of unconventional weapons.

> http://www.nytimes.com/2003/05/14/international/ worldspecial/14PENT.html?ex=10539361

Put simply, we don't know now and we didn't know before what WMD Iraq had.

> The Bush administration has changed its tune on Iraqi weapons of mass destruction, the reason it went to war there. Instead of looking for vast stocks of banned materials, it is now pinning its hopes on finding documentary evidence.

> http://www.nytimes.com/reuters/politics/politics-iraq-usa- weapons.html?ex=1053930535&ei...

The reason we went to war was because Iraq apparently had WMD, not documents about WMD. President Bush said on Oct. 7, 2002, "[t]he Iraqi regime…possesses and produces chemicals and biological weapons."

Perhaps most Americans won't care about this obvious dance to readjust the rug over history. The Gulf of Tonkin deception was not as well publicized and people could more easily be deceived. The WMD argument was made multiple times on national television. The UN didn't believe the President's WMD story, so the U.S. and Britain went off largely alone to remove a regime and destroy a country.

Our country was morally negligent, if not criminally negligent. We didn't trust in the system already set up to deter and monitor Saddam. We were consumed in our own self-righteousness at the exclusion of more temperate, wiser voices. I can only imagine right now that keeping our country in a high moral position is not a priority with our government. Yet, we have a President who constantly preaches Christian morality.

# May 15, 2003

Statistics unpublished until today reveal the stark fact: 242 people have died in Baghdad in just over three weeks, almost all from bullet wounds. It is an epidemic, and it is getting worse.

> http://news.independent.co.uk/world/midle_east/story.
> jsp?story=406657

Before the war, Baghdad had about one (1) murder per day, which was about the same statistic as Washington, DC or New York. I suppose if Baghdad were left to itself in the current anarchy, the killing would dry up on its own once no one is left to kill.

Right now we're discovering these terrible mass graves. These examples of Saddam's brutality are being used to replace the WMD arguments, but the killing continues in spite of Saddam. The perpetrator only now has a different face.

# May 17, 2003

The news revealed to us today yet another terrorist attack. Explosions ripped Morocco this time. Last week we saw Riyadh, Saudi Arabia get bombed.

The invasion of Iraq hasn't seemed to divert terrorism. Apparently terrorist groups were able to recoup their losses and begin a new offensive. The U.S.-Iraq war probably helped some fundamentalist organizations find new reasons to attack western congregations in these Arab countries.

The White House and Congress are probably aware that our Iraq adventure has created only a bigger monster in the Middle East, but I believe the political strategy is to look clueless because admitting to a terrible set of mistakes would be the kiss of death.

In the meantime we look stuck in Iraq. Apparently we won't be turning the country over to a provisional government anytime soon. I understand that Paul Bremer will act as the government authority for the foreseeable future. There's no audible debate in America right now over the terrible moral tragedy that our government has brought upon Iraq.

# May 18, 2003

Is it true that Condoleezza Rice said?:

> "Russia will be forgiven, but Germany will be ignored and
> France will be punished."

SJ Mercury
*Perspective*
5/18/03

I don't know the motives behind these countries' opposition to the Iraq war, but I do see them as now in the political position of appearing more prudent than the U.S. and UK.

Apparently Paul Bremer claims now that the Iraqi interim government is proceeding as planned. The news of a holdup in the transition process is false according to him. Now that we have conflicting reports we'll need to watch Iraq's evolution.

In spite of the continuing terror attacks in the Middle East, we hear that we're making significant progress in the war on terror. Bush says that about one-half of al-Qaeda has been eliminated. First, considering our intelligence services ability to gather accurate statistics, I don't know how we can know that we've diminished al-Qaeda by half when we can't locate the leader, Bin Laden.

This coming Tuesday our church will be packaging beans and rice for those in our community who are in need. Certainly I support this kind of giving. Our community needs to share more. My belief is that for many (perhaps most) of us wouldn't regularly eat beans and rice unless we absolutely had to. These staples are considered by many as underclass food. Our diet consists of meat and expensive, processed carbohydrates. Perhaps a more healthful diet would indeed consist of beans and rice. Perhaps if we all lived on combinations of grains and legumes, we would be healthier and less starvation and hunger would plague our planet.

# May 20, 2003

"We have had good evidence that there are literally thousands of al-Qaida trainees around," Porter Goss, chairman of the House Intelligence Committee, told ABC television. "And there is good reason to believe that some of those people are in the United States of America."

http://www.guardian.co.uk/alqaida/story/0,12469,958893,00.html

Did the Iraq war make a difference? No. We're at threat level orange (high) again. How can we believe that Bush is doing a good job protecting us against terrorism? Do we feel safer living in threat level orange? I imagine that if people's lives don't change, then whatever the government does or doesn't do makes no difference.

What a waste of energy Iraq is. Some say Saddam's atrocities over the years made the war worth the effort in spite of the WMD and the proliferation of these weapons to terrorists. Unfortunately if we were to stop Saddam's brutality, we should have tried to stop it before or during the occurrence. For example, we knew Saddam was slaughtering the Kurds and later the Shi'ites. Why didn't we do anything about these atrocities? Instead we spend our moral indignation on things like trying to impeach Clinton for sexual improprieties in the Oval Office. Dredging up Saddam's tortures now appears as a convenient ruse to distract us from the original reason (WMD) for the war.

# May 22, 2003

Senator Byrd – eighty-five years old – brings out some of the laundry that at least has been a stinking mess in my room.

> "Instead of addressing the contradictory evidence, the White House deftly changes the subject. No weapons of mass destruction have yet turned up, but we are told that they will in time.

> "It has raised serious questions about prevarication and reckless use of power. Were our troops needlessly put at risk? Were countless Iraqi civilians killed and maimed when war was not really necessary? Was the American public deliberately misled? Was the world?

> "It appears to this senator that the American people may have been lured into accepting the unprovoked invasion of a sovereign nation, in violation of long-standing international law, under false premises."

> http://www.nytimes.com/aponline/national/AP-Iraq-Byrd. html?ex=105456681&ei=1&en=6...

Only the oldest man in the Senate can tell the truth, or ask the questions that are roiling in many minds. The White House can only respond with:

> "It was widely known before the conflict began that Iraq possessed weapons of mass destruction, as was determined by the United Nations," White House spokeswoman Claire Buchan said. "In fact, we have already found at least

two mobile labs" suspected of being capable of producing biological weapons, she said.

But:

The Central Intelligence Agency has begun a review to try to determine if the American intelligence community erred in its prewar assessments of Saddam Hussein's government.

http://www.nytimes.com/2003/05/22/international/ worldspecial/22INTE.html?ex=10545723...

In the meantime:

The U.N. Security Council voted Thursday to lift sanctions against Iraq after almost 13 years and to give the United States and Great Britain authority to control the country until an elected government is in place.

http://www.cnn.com/2003/WORLD/meast/05/22/sprj.irq. main/index.html

But will the Iraqi people have their country back?

L. Paul Bremer III, the chief U.S. civilian in Iraq, said today that the selection of an interim Iraqi government is at least seven weeks away, prompting aspiring leaders from Kurdish and returned exile groups to warn that Iraqis are tiring of the six-week-old U.S. occupation and want swift movement toward self-rule.

http://www.washingtonpost.com/wp-dyn/articles/A18102-2003May21.html

EPA head Christie Whitman resigned yesterday. We can very clearly outline Bush's setback to environmental protection:

1.  Increased number of polluted waterways from 2000 to 2001;

2.  Toxic waste dump cleanups dropped 41%;

3.  Reduction in enforcement of pollution standards;

4.  Eased regulation that would require coal-fired power plants to install controls as these plants are expanded and modernized;

5.  Did not sign the Kyoto Treaty;

6.  Did not participate in WHO treaty to reduce proliferation of tobacco products.

Bush does little for the environment.

# *May 23, 2003*

I have focused on the WMD argument over the course of the Iraq war. To date no clear evidence is available to indicate if WMD exists or not. So far nothing has been found. I believe we can safely conclude that the U.S. began this war on a faulty premise. Enough evidence exists to question the President's legal legitimacy to carry out this war. The likelihood of a sufficient congressional majority to begin a serious proceeding against the President seems ridiculous. Just a small tide of concern is now appearing in Congress among Republicans. This concern is over the post-war efforts to bring stability back to Iraq.

> Richard Lugar, chairman of the Senate Foreign Relations Committee, said that Washington was in danger of creating "an incubator for terrorist cells and activity" unless it increased the scope and cost of its reconstruction efforts. He said that more troops, billions more dollars and a longer commitment were needed if the US were not to throw away the peace.
>
> http://www.timesonline.co.uk/article/0,,599-689407,00. html

At least these comments are being expressed by a Republican. Lugar, however, is a moderate. His comments met with some disagreement in the White House. Of course, Paul Wolfowitz thinks that Lugar's position creates a demand for perfection that can't be delivered. Of course, the question is what can be delivered.

> Afghanistan was the other disaster for America. We've essentially left this country behind.

> A small sample of Afghan civilians have shown "astonishing"
> levels of uranium in their urine, an independent scientist
> says.
>
> http://news.bbc.co.uk/2/hi/science/nature/3050317.stm

Of course, both the U.S. and UK deny that DU weapons were used in Afghanistan. Strange how the average urine sample contained 315.5 nanograms of uranium. The maximum permissible dose in the U.S. is 12 nanograms. Some of the people sampled displayed symptoms much like those of Gulf War veterans.

The Iraq war seemed amazingly short and did not present the major battlefield that some expected. The following could be the reason:

> Senior Iraqi officers who commanded troops crucial to
> the defence of key Iraqi cities were bribed not to fight by
> American special forces, the US general in charge of the
> war confirmed.
>
> http://news.independent.co.uk/world/middle_east/story.
> jsp?story=409090

The general here is Tommy Franks, who recently announced his retirement, even after receiving a Rumsfeld offer to become Joint Chief of the Army. I think he's tired of kissing up, and I don't think he actually agreed with our policy in Iraq. Unfortunately he didn't have the moral conviction to say no.

> Utah is getting ready to execute two convicted criminals
> by firing squad, an old and bloody means of execution that
> is likely to stir renewed debate about the cruelty of capital
> punishment in the United States.
>
> http://news.independent.co.uk/world/americas/story.
> jsp?story=408714

The first problem is we still use the death penalty. The second problem is we still have states using archaic methods of execution. But, perhaps this story says something about our country. Are we too quick to kill our own? Are we lax in our moral attitudes toward punishment? We clearly don't pay attention to the capital punishment issue. It is odd to me that the story about Utah didn't appear in the *Salt Lake Tribune* today. The story was run in the *NY Times*, the *SF Chronicle*, and several broadcast news companies.

# May 25, 2003

Along with destroying the lives and the environment of Afghanistan and Iraq, Bush continues to degrade the environment of his own country. *San Jose Mercury* reports today the Bush "has done less to expand the national parks system than any president in the last 100 years . . ." According to this article, every president has added an average of 2.4 new parks per year. Bush's average is 1.3. The budget for park repairs was cut 28% apparently to pay for an investigation to determine the feasibility of using private contractors rather than federal employees to maintain parks. The maintenance backlog is approaching 6- billion dollars. Park roads and facilities will likely never receive proper repair.

How can we beat Bush in 2004? Of course, the damage he's done is now irreparable.

# May 26, 2003

Today is Memorial Day. The government has set aside this day to remember the fallen soldiers of our many wars. I deeply regret that so many people have died, especially for causes that were questionable, or simply wrong. I hope we eventually understand and publish our foreign policies better so that everyone, especially our elected leaders can think them through. I hope our moral content puts the sacrifice of our youth at a position forbidden to access.

The tragedy of some of our recent wars is that the cause is brought about by a few select people supported by a compliant military, and generally tolerated by a powerless population. In the case of Iraq no check and balance existed for ignorance; and, ignorance drove us to war.

We know that the WMD status will never be fully resolved. Can we use Memorial Day to remember the foolish mistakes of an unelected president? Can we use Memorial Day to demand an accounting from the President explaining why he shouldn't be tried for criminal negligence that resulted in the deaths of over 100 American soldiers and thousands of Iraqi civilians?

*New York Times* columnist Tomas Friedman says the war was justified more by the mass graves of Shi'ite militia than the risk of WMD. This after-the-fact argument might work better if we forget that in 1991 the U.S. watched Saddam's army slaughter the rebelling Shi'ite forces. The basic truth is America didn't want an Islamic force to overthrow Saddam because we would have potentially another Iran on our hands. The U.S. put some dirt in those graves, but we couldn't get rid of the smell.

Obviously, I make no secret that Bush is a President delivered to us to help descend the world into ignorance and ill health.

Here's some statistics:

1. Oklahoma class sizes are in the 40's heading for the 50's because the state is cutting 6000 teaching jobs.

2. Oregon is closing schools several weeks early and laying-off public prosecutors to balance the budget.

3. Missouri has ordered the removal of every third light bulb to save energy costs.

4. 275,000 fewer Texans will receive health care this year.

5. Over this year and next 1.7 million Americans will be losing health insurance.

6. The No Child Left Behind Program is 40% under-funded.

http://www.guardian.co.uk/usa/story/0,12271,963529,00.html

The wars, the tax cuts, the devastated states, the destruction of the environment I hope are enough to prevent Bush from re-election. The American people were right the first time in not electing Bush. I hope we stay in the right in the next election.

# May 27, 2003

In the public's mind, the war may be over, but U.S. troops continue to fall in Iraq at the rate of one a day. That is down from an average of three a day between the start of the war on March19 and May 1 when a total of 139 American service members were killed.

http://www.msnbc.com/news/918152.asp?0c1=c3

The Pentagon apparently thinks that one death per day is normal, and, therefore, the military dismisses the statistic as a problem. Yet, we still haven't provided a reason why anyone should be dying in Iraq.

Republican Sen. Pat Roberts of Kansas, the Intelligence Committee Chairman, said he expected weapons to be found, and that the United States must make certain they have not fallen into the hands of terrorists or rogue nations.

If the weapons are not found, Roberts said on Meet the Press, "Basically, you have a real credibility problem."

http://asia.reuters.com/newsArticle.jhtml?type=politicsNews&storyID=2814182

I think the problem is greater than credibility. I think the Iraq calamity falls into the area of criminal negligence and war crimes. People are still dying for God knows what.

# May 28, 2003

Last Sunday I disconnected my television from the cable service and power and moved it out of my sight. I haven't watched it since. The content was totally empty and the news is about the same. I now find myself reading a bit more.

When I read the *SJ Mercury* yesterday about more companies moving off shore to avoid corporate taxes, while at the same time obtaining large federal contracts, I concluded that maybe we all should engage in this tax avoidance scheme. For example, we could all form small corporations offshore. Then we higher ourselves out as contractors to perform work in the U.S. Could we avoid paying corporate taxes that way? Perhaps we could ask for payment in cash or barter: anything to avoid taxes? I noted that a spin-off of Arthur Anderson has incorporated offshore and this company has a very large federal contract—almost one-billion dollars. These companies don't seem to be constrained by country loyalty.

Today's Mercury has a story about Andrew Liersen, ex-president of Goodwill Industries in Santa Clara County. This individual is facing charges of looting Goodwill of several million dollars. He ran from the law and ended up being expelled from Guatemala for money laundering. He's now in U.S. custody.

These two stories about American companies bring me back to our policy in Iraq, which represents a condition of legal disregard on the part of our government. The attitude seems to be that if the legal approach through the UN doesn't work, disregard it. The process of disregard is to connive by creating a fraudulent emergency in the name of WMD, and then we commence to rob the American coffers to support a war that ultimately benefits the oil industry and other cronies involved in post war reconstruction. The interesting aspect of this sociopathism is that nothing happens to the perpetrators, nor do these perpetrators act as though they've made a mistake or experience any shame. Certainly I won't be able to talk anybody into feeling shame for our foreign policy, but I will take the blame for having higher expectations for our leaders.

# May 29, 2003

Below in chronological order is the exchange of emails to Utah's Governor regarding the firing squad execution sentence:

From: "Rounds, Frederic"
< 05/23/03 05:34PM >>>
To: Governor of Utah

If we must have capital punishment, let's at least outlaw firing squads. I find the idea of a firing squad barbaric and to ask a group of people to perform this killing seems morally archaic.thanks,

Fred Rounds

From: Jack Ford, Assistant to the Governor of Utah

Sent: Wednesday, May 28, 2003 11:37 AM

To: Rounds, Frederic

Subject: Re: firing squad

The Governor is in agreement. The statute is still on the books that allows the condemned man to chose between firing squad and lethal injection. Firing squad is less barbaric than electric chair and gas chamber and it is instantaneous.

I'm speechless. No one has ever had a serious conversation with me regarding the advantages of a firing squad over other means of execution.

Well, at least the Governor is in agreement—I think—that firing squads are an outmoded form of capital punishment. Maybe that's progress.

I noticed a story in the *SJ Mercury* today that Utah is now looking for a group of sharpshooters to staff the firing squad. I wonder if Utah has asked the White House.

Bush signed the $350-billion tax bill yesterday, while simultaneously the debt ceiling was raised to $7.4-trillion. The bill provides $20-billion for the states. Unfortunately California's debt now exceeds $30-billion. And, this $20-billion must be divided among all the other states, including Texas which has a debt of $10-billion. So, I'm expecting a tax cut from the Feds, but tax increases from the states. I expect services within the states to be substantially reduced.

> Mr. Rumsfeld ignited the row in a speech in New York, declaring: "It is ... possible that they [Iraq] decided that they would destroy them prior to a conflict and I don't know the answer."
>
> http://news.independent.co.uk/world/politics/story.jsp?story=410484

Excuse me, Mr. Rumsfeld, but are you saying that Iraq may have disposed of the WMD before the war? What's wrong with our intelligence? Did you hype the WMD problem in order to scare the world into a conflict?

Tony Blair says that he has "no doubt" that Iraq had a WMD program. No one has any doubt that Saddam once had a program, but the question is when the program of weapons production and storage ended. Note that Rumsfeld states the possibility that the WMD were destroyed before the war. How long before the war? Years? All the evidence presented so far points to the condition that the WMD was destroyed years before.

Do we have a case of incompetence, manipulation of intelligence, or both? Where are the impeachment proceedings?

# May 30, 2003

The evidence for WMD is a lie.

Britain's dossier on Iraq's weapons of mass destruction was rewritten on orders from Prime Minister Tony Blair's government to make it look more dramatic in the months leading up to the U.S.-led war against Baghdad, a top intelligence official said Thursday.

> http://www.upi.com/view.cfm?StoryID=20030529-102724-2960r

> "For bureaucratic reasons we settled on one issue, weapons of mass destruction, because it was the one reason everyone could agree on," Mr. Wolfowitz tells the magazine.

> http://news.independent.co.uk/world/middle_east/story.jsp?story=410730

People are coming out of the woodwork now: Rumsfeld and Wolfowitz, for example. They seem to be admitting to exaggerating the real WMD threat. Of course, neither Rumsfeld, nor Wolfowitz seem particularly worried that quite a few people have died over their unconscionable behavior.

> "The truth is that for reasons that have a lot to do with the U.S. government bureaucracy, we settled on the one issue that everyone could agree on which was weapons of mass destruction as the core reason," Wolfowitz was quoted as saying in a Pentagon transcript of an interview with Vanity Fair.

> "Have a little patience," he said in Warsaw, Poland. "I have absolutely no doubt at all that we will present the full

evidence after we have investigated all the sites, after we've interviewed all the scientists and experts, and this will take place in the coming weeks and months."

http://www.nytimes.com/apoline/international/AP-Wolfowitz-Iraq.html

The above shows two ways in which Wolfowitz was quoted. Neither makes much sense, other than admitting that we didn't have any solid argument for going to war, but WMD is the most terrifying so for "bureaucratic" reasons we picked that. As to whether any actual threat existed seems immaterial.

Now Wolfowitz wants us to have patience, so we can eventually put together the WMD story. Times up, Mr. Wolfowitz. We apparently knew before the war that WMD existed and was ready to be deployed in 45 minutes. Now those original allegations haven't materialized into reality and a great deal of damage has been done to innocent people. The criminal mistake has been committed. All we can do now is make reparations and experience the loss to the world.

# May 31, 2003

Part of the ridiculous argument involving WMD is that the quantities that our President and others said existed in Iraq were based on old information obtained after the first Gulf war. Under ideal conditions VX nerve agent has a half-life of 350 days. When VX is weaponized, the half-life is shortened considerably. After five years of storage, none of the existing arsenal of chemical agents would retain much effectiveness.

Anthrax spores on the other hand can be stored for many years. Supposedly Iraq has 8500 liters of this poison sitting around. For the spores to be effective the containment must be kept very dry. The only effective way to eliminate Anthrax is burning or steam decontamination. 8500 liters of Anthrax—though sounding like a large amount—would fill about 80, 50-gallon drums. This stock pile would be relatively easy to find, if distributed to armories for actual use in weapons. But, weapons grade Anthrax has never been found in any of Iraq's armories. As for the apparent bio-weapons trailers, these are capable of producing about one liter per month.

Hence, these mobile laboratories could never produce the Anthrax volume described by the White House. In addition, if Iraq had 8500 liters of Anthrax, no real need would exist to produce more. Under ideal conditions 8500 liters of Anthrax is sufficient to kill millions of people.

> "Believe me, its not for lack of trying. We've been to virtually every ammunition supply point between the Kuwaiti border and Baghdad, but they're simply not there," Conway [commander of the 1st Marine Expeditionary Force] said.
>
> Bush, however, told a Polish television network: "We found the weapons of mass destruction. We found biological

246

laboratories…and we'll find more weapons as time goes on. But for those who say we haven't found the banned devices or banned weapons, we have found them."

SJ Mercury

5/31/03

Now, Mr. President, the biological laboratories are not weapons. I imagine we'll give the President ample time to find the WMD if it exists. But, I continue to remind myself that the experts who should know about the WMD in Iraq continue with the story that the weapons were destroyed. The President is blathering when he speaks about the existence of WMD. At this point nothing believable comes from his mouth. He's lost all credibility. Bush appears to be a puppet of reactionary extremists who have somehow infiltrated the halls of government, and our checks and balances have failed us.

# June 2, 2003

"Our case was a very clear and explicit one," Mr. Straw said.

Ms Short, Mr Cook and others were "trying to change the basis on which those judgments were made," he said.

"We never said that we are proposing to take military action on a contingency of what we might find in the future.

"I hope very much we do find further evidence, but it will be further evidence."

http://politics.guardian.co.uk/iraq/ story/0,12956,968826,00.html

No, Mr. Straw, you can't find any of evidence of what you said Iraq had in the past. You said Iraq had a current capability to use and produce WMD. Now where is it? Was it dismantled while the inspectors were there? Your case, Mr. Straw, clearly failed and the results have been disastrous. Why is there no shame? What do you hope to gain by continuing the spread of misinformation?

# June 3, 2003

The evidence that has passed through the news clearly shows that the U.S. preemptively invaded a sovereign nation based on inaccurate intelligence regarding the extent of Saddam's WMD. Iraq clearly did not have the stockpiles that the White House reported, nor did she have production facilities to produce these weapons quickly.

Every aspect of the intelligence information has proved to be wrong and in some circumstances fake. The U.S. did not have the locations of any WMD storage or manufacturing facility.

The problem that stands out is the idea of preemption. I suppose one could argue that regime change may be valid if a real threat exists beyond doubt. In the case of Iraq the threat was based on faulty data and unverified intelligence. War proceeded even after some of Colin Powell's information was declared bogus by UNMOVIC. What surprises me is that no one in our government became very suspicious about Powell's information immediately after Inspector Baradei challenged the Secretary of State's claims. Clearly when the Powell's WMD argument started to falter so did the justification for preemptive war. What happened to our sense of truth and ethical procedure? Does our government really feel it can do whatever it wants in the world with no consequences?

At present no evidence exists that implies that intelligence was manipulated to achieve a political objective. We may never understand the full logic behind our invasion of Iraq. I am suspicious that most of our Congress and the White House wanted to rid the world of Saddam. The existence of WMD is immaterial. I believe Diane Feinstein feels that Saddam needed removal and just about any reason would be sufficient. She's not showing much concern about the credibility gulf now opening widely in Washington.

What I see are shades being pulled over the WMD issue. People are asking questions, but the strategy is to answer them with just about any sort of spin just to pacify the issue until people tire of it.

Hopefully the rhetoric bubbling up over Iran's nuclear enterprise won't get us involved in another war. I hope we've learned what information is trustworthy.

# June 4, 2003

Here's another story about Paul Wolfowitz:

> Asked why a nuclear power such as North Korea was being
> treated differently from Iraq, where hardly any weapons of
> mass destruction had been found, the deputy defence minister
> said: "Let's look at it simply. The most important difference
> between North Korea and Iraq is that economically, we just
> had no choice in Iraq. The country swims on a sea of oil."
>
> http://www.guardian.co.uk/Iraq/Stroy/0,2763,970331,00.
> html

The war in Iraq apparently was an important target because of oil.
Somebody ought to shut Wolfowitz up. He's just a bit too honest for
Washington. At any rate with comments like the one above, Bush and crowd
are finished. At least Wolfowitz seems to be blatantly and cavalierly honest.

# *June 6, 2003*

The Guardian retracted the story quoting the Wolfowitz comment regarding oil [ see my June 5, 2003 notes ] as the true basis for the war. What Wolfowitz apparently said was:

> "Look, the primary difference—to put it too simply— between North Korea and Iraq is that we had virtually no economic options with Iraq because the country floats on a sea of oil. In the case of North Korea, the country is teetering on the edge of economic collapse and that I believe is a major point of leverage whereas the military picture with North Korea is very different from that with Iraq. The problems in both cases have some similarities but the solutions have got to be tailored to the circumstances which are very different.
>
> http://www.guardian.co.uk/corrections/ story/0.3604,971436,00.html

I don't think this corrected version of Wolfowitz's statement makes me feel any better. The logic means that economic and military conditions dictate whether we go to war or not. Wolfowitz is saying that because Iraq had wealth in oil the only viable way to force political change is through war. I believe Wolfowitz also implies that Iraq was weak militarily; therefore war was more feasible with Iraq than with North Korea which has a better developed military. I thought we went to war because Saddam presented an imminent threat to our national security. Under such circumstances wouldn't we need to go to war in spite of an enemy's economic and/or military conditions?

President Bush, in Qatar, yesterday, said: "We'll reveal the truth. But one thing is certain: no terrorist network will gain weapons of mass destruction form the Iraqi regime, because it is no more."

http://www.guardian.co.uk/Iraq/Story/0,2663,9715786,00.
html

Unfortunately, Bush might be too late. The Tuwaitha nuclear waste storage site has already been looted. Potential terrorists may already have walked away with materials to make a dirty bomb. And, since we can't find any other WMD, maybe these poisonous agents have already been spirited into the hands of evil doers. These WMD would be worth a lot of money in the terrorist market. Bush's threat of war may have been the catalyst for Saddam to dump his WMD into the hands of other dangerous parties. So, Bush's policies could have caused the very thing he is afraid of.

## June 7, 2003

Reuters and the *San Jose Mercury* both reported today that the Defense Intelligence Agency published a report that reveals considerable doubt in Iraq's WMD. Clearly again, the flow of information was perturbed as it entered the hands of Powell and Bush. Members of Congress are beginning to ask questions, but Senator Byrd appears as the only one stating what to me is obvious: where's the moral outrage over what the President has done? Of course, if someone doesn't feel the outrage, talking that person into it is generally impossible. Hence, Bush will likely survive this preemption policy, and we will have four more years of him.

# June 10, 2003

Bush now back peddles when he speaks about WMD. He doesn't talk about Iraq having any current stash of WMD. He says Saddam had an ongoing WMD program right up to the start of the war. He isn't mentioning the two mobile labs anymore, since so much controversy exists about them. He continues to say that WMD will be found after looking, even though search teams claim they have no further places to inspect.

Condoleezza Rice says that thousands of documents and many Iraqis need examination before any conclusion can be drawn about Iraq's WMD. The idea, I suppose, is to drag this issue out for as long as possible. If Bush just continues to say the WMD will be found, then eventually people will give up, or Congress will vote for some investigation. Bush will slide right through the WMD-gate.

How could we nearly impeach a President for extramarital affairs, but then do nothing with a president who manipulates us into an unnecessary war. I could write Senator Feinstein regarding what appears to be a severe moral inconsistency, but I don't think she sees Iraq as an important issue. I've actually written her five times in the recent past. I have received the same form letter reply also five times.

# June 11, 2003

Senator Roberts, head of the Foreign Relations Committee, said he has seen no evidence [www.cnn.com, 6/11/03] that WMD was manipulated to create strong justification for war. However, he did say that CIA officials admitted that they were under pressure to "skew their analysis."

We must keep in mind that the information from the CIA ultimately ends up as reports to the President. So, I would say that we have a cycle of manipulation here. Actually what is pressure to "skew their analysis" really mean? Is making a mountain out of a mole hill skewing the analysis?

Now this same Foreign Relations Committee would not agree to a formal investigation of WMD intelligence. The Democrats wanted a formal investigation. The Republicans said that nothing formal should be done at this time other than routine procedures.

How does Monica Lewinsky rate a Ken Starr and Bush merely gets a routine and probably perfunctory scoping?

> "United Nations inspections also revealed that Iraq likely maintains stockpiles of VX, mustard, and other chemical agents, and that the regime is rebuilding and expanding facilities capable of producing chemical weapons…
>
> Should Iraq acquire fissile material it would be able to build a nuclear weapons within a year."
>
> President Bush
> 9/12/02

> "The inspections are not working."
>
> President Bush

3/6/03
"Intelligence by this and other governments leaves no doubt
that the Iraq regime continues to possess and conceal some of
the most lethal weapons ever devised."


President Bush
3/17/03

In the six months between September, 2002 and March, 2003 Bush was convinced that since the UN Inspectors hadn't found anything, the inspection process was a failure. Blix was apparently incompetent. Bush proclaimed without doubt that Iraq had the WMD, even though the U.S. had supplied her intelligence to the UN inspection team. I note also that American special forces teams situated in Iraq before the war began were also unable to locate any stores of WMD.

And the story proceeds as we fail to find WMD. Bush continues to tell the world that the illegal weapons are buried somewhere in a country the size of California. I think that the people hearing the monotonous Bush rhetoric are losing interest.

Clearly Bush exaggerated—intentionally or not—the WMD dangers. He was recklessly incautious with the intelligence.

Why aren't we outraged?

Rob Elder [*SJ Mercury*, 6/11/03] answers this question:

1. "Americans are too busy to bother with the details."

2. Bush is "very adept at justifying his actions by invoking traditional American values that satisfy our emotions, ..."

The Associated Press reported today that 3240 civilians were killed in the Iraq war.

# June 12, 2003

I wrote the following letter to Senator Pat Roberts, chair of the Intelligence Committee:

> I believe the hearings on Iraq's WMD intelligence should be formal and public.

> We nearly brought impeachment proceedings on President Clinton because of sexual improprieties. To remain consistent I don't understand how our faulty intelligence can be relegated to "routine" scrutiny. After all, 3200 innocent civilians were killed during the Iraq war and American soldiers are still dying almost daily. Apparently our intelligence about Iraq's WMD is what led us into this war. If Clinton's impeachment hearings weren't routine, how could we possibly consider the issue of our failed intelligence to be routine? Clinton's behavior didn't result in an American military invasion.

> In addition, we knew the intelligence being fed to Powell and Bush was faulty well before the invasion. The uranium fiasco with Niger was refuted within a week after Powell presented it. And, none of the U.S. intelligence being fed to UNSCOM led to any discoveries. And, the Special Forces teams inside Iraq before the war also found nothing. The mobile labs that Bush quickly jumped on recently are most likely for hydrogen production and were supplied by the British in 1987. Please remember that inspections for WMD

began last November, 2002. In the last eight months of searching we have found nothing. Are you saying that for a President and Secretary of State to knowingly use this faulty intelligence to justify a war is routine? How many times did President Bush use the aluminum tube argument? The answer is multiple times, even after the world knew that the use for these tubes as uncertain.

Please open your hearings.
Sincerely,
Fred Rounds

# June 13, 2003

Buried in the news media today is a story that describes how the CIA informed the White House in March, 2002 that the Niger-Iraq-uranium story was bogus. MSNBC and the *SJ Mercury* both carried this story while simultaneously reporting our latest raid on a town 90 miles north of Baghdad. Maybe around 100 Iraqi fighters were killed. No Americans died. Even though Bush declared the war over, we're still fighting.

The *Guardian* ran a story today about the number of civilians killed during the Iraq war. The group, Iraq Body Count, consisting of U.S. and UK researchers quoted a number between 5000 and 7000, but this number may grow to 10,000 as the group completes its activity. I can now imagine Saddam's graveyards of Iraqi thousands alongside ours of more Iraqi thousands.

Where are we? Are we lost in this mess? Reason and morality seem to have abandoned our minds. Everything to date adds to the overwhelming conclusion that this war in Iraq was cooked up. But, I don't understand the reason behind the effort that got us into Iraq. Clearly WMD wasn't the real reason for this war. If oil were the reason, then we could have obtained this resource without going to war. What about the son trying to complete the unfinished business of his Father. How could a majority of Congress get behind the idea emanating from a child's longings?

In the end, maybe no reason exists and to search for one may be only an endless road towards an unfulfilled obsession. Perhaps no rationale exists.

Congressman Waxman asked Condoleezza Rice why the President used the bogus story about Nigerian uranium. She seems to be of the belief, however, that "no one in our circles knew that there were doubts and suspicions..." [*SJ Mercury*, 6/13/03]. Maybe she didn't know.

Apparently the White House learned that the uranium story was bogus from the *New York Times* columnist, Nicolas Kristof [ NYT, Op-Ed, 6/13/03]. Under the leadership of Dick Cheney, the Niger connection was investigated early in 2002 only to reveal the story lacked credibility.

By early March, 2003, however, the entire world knew the uranium story was bogus. Why didn't this revelation raise a red flag in the White House? Why wasn't the CIA raked over the coals for feeding the President bogus information?

I am projecting my own emotions regarding my integrity when I ask these questions. I would find myself embarrassed if I had presented to the world bogus information that ultimately resulted in a war, and I would be livid beyond belief if I found out later that my information sources knowingly gave me fake information. I would feel set up. I'm mystified why Dick Cheney didn't communicate to the President the results of the Niger investigation that he ordered.

The fact that no shakeup occurred within the CIA leads me to believe that Bush and Powell both knew full well that some or even all their intelligence was at best doubtful and probably just plain wrong. But, this conclusion stems from my suspicious mind.

# June 17, 2003

I punish myself when I lose energy for an important subject. Unfortunately I'm losing a lot of energy regarding the Iraq issues. I suppose our politicians are hoping people will eventually lose interest, so that the problem won't crop up around election time. In my own mind Iraq is the biggest fiasco the President has gotten us into, but this feeling of mine seems out of sync with the rest of America.

I read a recent poll that states that 60 percent of Americans believe Saddam had something to do with 9/11. Of course, not a shred of evidence exists to make such a claim. But, this large percentage is enough to elect a President or start a war. I'm still mystified as to how so many of us remain uninformed.

However, the pollsters and election analysts tend to develop a detailed understanding of how people feel about issues. Consequently, I imagine the Bush Administration feels pretty safe right now with only a minority taking notice of the information about Iraq's WMD.

Senator Roberts takes a hokum attitude about investigating our intelligence. "Routine," he calls it, as if we occupy another country every day.

I have been brought to question my values continuously during this presidency. I feel that aspects of our government's behavior appear as roguish and out of control. I don't want to be part of the current political philosophy, and I want more leaders to accept a moderate relationship with the rest of the world. Yet, I feel trapped because I see no competition for this presidency.

The Republicans are raising hundreds-of-millions of dollars for the re-election campaigns. The Democrats are nowhere near this dollar value and whatever money the Democrats raise must be spread over nine candidates.

Is what I'm seeing a passing phase in politics? Was our politics always like this, but we were never given the chance to notice?

# June 27, 2003

I was hoping that by this point we would see some progress in bringing peace to Iraq. Unfortunately the conditions there grow worse. A soldier dies almost every day. At least one or more Iraqi civilians die there every day often from American bullets. WMD has not been found, except for documents and equipment that mostly relate to events that took place ten or more years ago. The White House isn't bothered by its past inconsistencies over what led us up to this war and the Congress isn't aggressively trying to balance the power. The American people seem not to care whether the White House told the truth or not. Saddam is gone. We won. Enough said. People are now back to work or looking for work. Iraq is history and we can't see the Iraqis and Americans dying.

I thought I would have some comments to make at this point. What comes to mind is the ancient Greek play Lysistrata which is playing all over America right now. The intent is to make an antiwar statement using theater as a vehicle. Perhaps putting on an old play is more creative than shouting in the streets. But, how many will listen to the words of Aristophanes (died 385 b.c.e.)? The play tells a good story about women who grow tired of seeing their husbands continually torn away by war. So, they decide to withhold sex until the warriors make peace. Of course, the play is a comedy, but perhaps some moral message might exist for Laura Bush.

I was looking for some deeper message buried in the Peloponnesian history. Most assuredly a message does exist, since Athens decided to break from peace and invade Sicily. Even though Athens had a great Army and Navy, she suffered a devastating loss. The Spartans then took advantage of Athens' weakened state and they came in for the kill with the help of angry Persians.

The lesson for me is that great militaries can be defeated. The Athenians were confident in their military strength, but they were defeated through the tactic of surprise. America indeed has the most powerful military in the world, but again the surprise tactics of guerrilla and terrorist warfare drain the blood and resources from the American enterprise. America lost Vietnam completely on the basis of surprise, but not surprise in the military sense. America was surprised that a small country could hold on to its mission year after year, even after she was defeated in battles over and over again.

Ultimately America lost Vietnam because she lost the most important source of power behind the fight: the truth or the reason for the war in the first place. No one could convincingly articulate the reason for Vietnam anymore, but thousands of people were still dying. Everyone at the time knew the war had to end, but we had to save face. Vietnam let us retain some of our egos, until we had pulled all our troops out. By that point no one really cared what happened to Vietnam.

Athens and Vietnam were generations ago. Our ancestors got us into these wars. Many dutiful and good people fought in these adventures, including myself (Vietnam). Somehow, however, we keep getting sucked in to new wars, and no rescuer—like Lysistrata—comes along to pull us out.

# January 13, 2005

After thousands have died and a country ruined and in chaos, the final WMD report came to light yesterday: Iraq didn't have WMD before the war started. The active search has been called off. The current leading weapons inspector, Charles A. Duefler, has completed his search program. He basically confirmed what Donald Kay reported a year ago. Saddam had destroyed his WMD in the early 1990's. [See http://www.nytimes.com/2005/01/12 ] He basically confirmed what Saddam and all the other Iraqis had said before the war began. He confirmed what the UN inspection teams under Hans Blix had been finding months before Bush dropped bombs on Baghdad. Duefler confirmed what many others and I were thinking during the entire course of Bush's bellicosity. Bush and his neoconservative cronies fabricated a drama of death and destruction based on melting snow resting above a deep crevasse. The snow melted rather quickly and now the U.S. and the "willing" partners have fallen in.

What does Bush say to all this:

> In an interview with ABC television's Barbara Walters, Mr Bush admitted: "I felt like we'd find weapons of mass destruction, or like many many here in the United States, many around the world, the United Nations, thought he had weapons of mass destruction."

> But asked directly whether the invasion of Iraq was worth the cost of an increasingly violent war, Mr Bush said: "Oh, absolutely."

http://www.guardian.co.uk/international/
story/0,3604,1389145,00.html

I can sum up Bush's response as, "Woops, I thought they had WMD."
Who are the "many", Mr. Bush? Perhaps many did think WMD existed in
Iraq, but also many believed the evidence wasn't sufficient to start a war over:
China, Germany, France, Russia, Mexico, Canada, the Vatican, 80% of the
population of the UK. You, Bush, went to war without UN support. We led
a coalition of the willing in spite of many calls for restraint.

I wonder how Bush got himself reelected. I didn't think the American
people could possibly be convinced that Bush has done good things for the
country. How poor I am in judging the voting population. The voters
were right in 2000. What happened in 2004? Greg Palast and others think
the voting was rigged in places like Ohio and Florida. The 2004 election
in November was filled with anecdotal stories of broken electronic voting
machines, long lines at the polls, unwillingness to count provisional ballots,
people being turned away because of registration issues, and so on. But,
nothing clear has come forward that indicates the election was rigged, even
though the anecdotes that I heard about seemed to favor Republicans for the
most part.

However, I find myself thinking that Senator John Kerry didn't offer a
significant difference when considering the Iraq war. As a matter of fact, he
advocated increasing the number of troops. He reminded me of Lyndon
Johnson during the Vietnam War. I could imagine the American people
thinking that since Kerry didn't present a clear exit strategy, we might as well
let the person who broke Iraq fix it.

> Thirty-five years ago I was carried off to a war that was
> conjured up with a bogus story about an American destroyer
> being shot at in the Gulf of Tonkin. Almost sixty-thousand
> soldiers died in Vietnam and over one-million Vietnamese.
> The memory of that war is in almost every American's
> head that lived through the 1960's and 70's. Most of our
> government leaders are in this group. What happened? How
> did we get to this place having experienced the trauma of the
> past? How can we sit and watch a President who responds
> with "Oh, absolutely?" Where is the shame for a terrible
> mistake? Where is our moral indignation and outrage?